Scarecrow Studies in Young Adult Literature
Series Editor: Patty Campbell

Scarecrow Studies in Young Adult Literature is intended to continue the body of critical writing established in Twayne's Young Adult Authors Series and to expand it beyond single-author studies to explorations of genres, multicultural writing, and controversial issues in young adult (YA) reading. Many of the contributing authors of the series are among the leading scholars and critics of adolescent literature, and some are YA novelists themselves.

The series is shaped by its editor, Patty Campbell, who is a renowned authority in the field, with a thirty-year background as critic, lecturer, librarian, and teacher of YA literature. Patty Campbell was the 2001 winner of the ALAN Award, given by the Assembly on Adolescent Literature of the National Council of Teachers of English for distinguished contribution to YA literature. In 1989 she was the winner of the American Library Association's Grolier Award for distinguished service to young adults and reading.

1. *What's So Scary about R. L. Stine?* by Patrick Jones, 1998.
2. *Ann Rinaldi: Historian and Storyteller*, by Jeanne M. McGlinn, 2000.
3. *Norma Fox Mazer: A Writer's World*, by Arthea J. S. Reed, 2000.
4. *Exploding the Myths: The Truth about Teens and Reading*, by Marc Aronson, 2001.
5. *The Agony and the Eggplant: Daniel Pinkwater's Heroic Struggles in the Name of YA Literature*, by Walter Hogan, 2001.
6. *Caroline Cooney: Faith and Fiction*, by Pamela Sissi Carroll, 2001.
7. *Declarations of Independence: Empowered Girls in Young Adult Literature, 1990–2001*, by Joanne Brown and Nancy St. Clair, 2002.
8. *Lost Masterworks of Young Adult Literature*, by Connie S. Zitlow, 2002.
9. *Beyond the Pale: New Essays for a New Era*, by Marc Aronson, 2003.
10. *Orson Scott Card: Writer of the Terrible Choice*, by Edith S. Tyson, 2003.
11. *Jacqueline Woodson: "The Real Thing,"* by Lois Thomas Stover, 2003.

Karen Hesse

Rosemary Oliphant-Ingham

*Scarecrow Studies in Young Adult
Literature, No. 19*

The Scarecrow Press, Inc.
Lanham, Maryland • Toronto • Oxford
2005

SCARECROW PRESS, INC.

Published in the United States of America
by Scarecrow Press, Inc.
A wholly owned subsidiary of
The Rowman & Littlefield Publishing Group, Inc.
4501 Forbes Boulevard, Suite 200, Lanham, Maryland 20706
www.scarecrowpress.com

PO Box 317
Oxford
OX2 9RU, UK

British Library Cataloguing in Publication Information Available

Library of Congress Cataloging-in-Publication Data

Oliphant-Ingham, Rosemary, 1943–
  Karen Hesse / Rosemary Oliphant-Ingham.
    p. cm. — (Scarecrow studies in young adult literature ; no. 19)
  Includes bibliographical references (p.) and index.
  ISBN 0-8108-5391-4 (alk. paper)
  1. Hesse, Karen—Criticism and interpretation. 2. Young adult fiction,
American—History and criticism. I. Title. II. Scarecrow studies in young adult
literature ; 19.

  PS3558.E797867Z84 2005
  813'.54—dc22

                                                                      2004027767

For Nan and Cecil Oliphant
and Jim Ingham

For my former, present, and future readers of
children's and adolescent literature:

Graham and Erik Barker
Madison and Mary Dade Ford
Chris Queen
Jameson Cook
Will and Sam Larson

Contents

Acknowledgments

This book could not have been written without the assistance and support of numerous people. Thanks to Richard F. Abrahamson for introducing me to children's and adolescent literature, Karen Hesse for her wonderful books and for graciously responding in a timely manner to numerous emails, Patty Campbell for encouragement and fantastic editing, Barbara (Bobbi) Samuels for listening to ideas and brainstorming better ones, Ann Oliphant Cook for reading and correcting drafts, Mary Frances Phenicie for research assistance, Patrick Wilcher and Katie Ellis Simmons for all the things outstanding graduate assistants do, Tomiko Mackey for being such a good listener, and Farrah Miller for formatting and typing talents. Also, to my "family" for love, support, and encouragement: Joe Larson, Jim Cook, Carolyn and Van Oliphant, Celia and Norman Ford, Renee and Alan Queen, Kristi and Jay Cook, Ingrid and Roger Barker, and Brent and Christy Larson.

Chronology

1952: August 29, Karen Donald born in Baltimore, Maryland, to parents Frances (Broth) and Alvin Donald, older brother, Mark

1962: Fifth grade teacher, Mrs. Datnoff, encourages her writing

1963: Sixth grade teacher, Mr. Ball, also offers encouragement

1969: Graduates from Pikesville High School. Enrolls at Towson State College (University)

1970: Enrolls at the University of Maryland (College Park)

1971: Marries Randy Hesse

1975: Graduates from the University of Maryland (College Park)

1976: Randy and Karen tent camp across America

1979: April 11, daughter Kate is born

1982: May 7, daughter Rachel is born

1985: Submits first manuscript

1991: Writes first book, *Wish on a Unicorn*

1992: Writes *Letters from Rifka*

1993: Writes *Poppy's Chair, Lavender,* and *Lester's Dog*

1994: Writes *Sable* and *Phoenix Rising*

1995: Writes *A Time of Angels*

1996: Writes *The Music of Dolphins*

1997: Writes *Out of the Dust*

1998: *Out of the Dust* is awarded the John Newbery Medal from the American Library Association

1999: Writes *Come On, Rain, A Light in the Storm: The Civil War Diary of Amelia Martin* (Dear America Series), and *Just Juice*

2000: Writes *Stowaway*

2001: Writes *Witness*

2002: Is awarded a MacArthur Genius Fellowship

2003: Writes *The Stone Lamp: Eight Stories of Hanukkah through History*

Introduction

Karen Hesse Is a Genius!

When she was a child, several teachers recognized it in her writing and encouraged it. Her readers have known it since 1991 when *Wish on a Unicorn* was published. The Newbery committee recognized it when they awarded *Out of the Dust* the 1998 Newbery Medal. Her publisher, Brenda Bowen, at Simon & Schuster said, "I always thought she was a genius. I'm glad to have it confirmed."[1]

The official confirmation of Karen Hesse's genius status comes from The John D. and Catherine T. MacArthur Foundation. In 2002 this group honored Hesse with the prestigious "Genius Fellows Award." The only other writer of literature for children and young adults to receive this honor prior to 2002 was Virginia Hamilton, who was named a fellow in 1995. (In 2003 Angela Johnson and Peter Sis joined this prestigious duo.) The MacArthur Fellows Program awards these fellowships to people who have shown extraordinary originality and dedication in their creative pursuits—people who "lift our spirits, illuminate human potential, and shape our collective future."[2] The committee specifically acknowledged Karen Hesse for "expanding the possibilities of literature for children and young adults."[3] Along with the honor of being named a Genius Fellow, a significant monetary award allows the winner to pursue creative, intellectual, and professional inclinations without having to worry about marketability of the works created. The MacArthur Genius Fellowships are an investment in originality, insight, and potential. Readers of Karen Hesse's books know that she fits all of the above criteria. With typical modesty, she accepted this award for her entire profession when she said, "I just hope that this brings recognition to the entire field of children's literature."[4]

Hesse's originality shines in the free verse poetry format of *Out of the Dust*, as well as in the format she uses in *The Stone Lamp: Eight Stories of Hanukkah through History* to show a time line of Jewish history—a page giving the history of a specific historical event followed by a Hanukkah story from that period. She uses drama to show how a small Vermont town in the 1920s responds to the KKK's attempts to become a part of the community. Even her agent was a little surprised to hear about a story of nuclear disaster for the young adult reader, but Hesse pulled it off in *Phoenix Rising*. In order to show Mila's language development in *The Music of Dolphins*, Hesse makes striking use of syntax and gradations of font size to represent Mila's language and thought processes throughout the story. A ship's log tells Nicholas Young's story about his journey with Captain James Cook on that famous exploratory voyage on the *Endeavour*.

For Hesse the Genius Fellow award is yet one more accolade added to a list that covers several pages. During her brief career, Hesse has won the Newbery Award, the 1998 Scott O'Dell Award for Historical Fiction, two Christopher Awards, and numerous awards from the American Library Association, the International Reading Association, the National Council of Teachers of English, *Horn Book, School Library Journal, Booklist, Book Links, Publisher's Weekly*, The New York Public Library, and several children's choices state awards.

Webster's Dictionary defines genius as someone with extraordinary intellectual power in creative ability and someone who influences others for good.[5] Karen Hesse definitely fits this definition. The author of seventeen books and one short story for children and young adults, Hesse's intelligence and creativity shine in all her works.

Notes

1. "Karen Hesse Awarded MacArthur Fellowship," Simon & Schuster Publishing, NY, September 25, 2002.

2. Debra Lau Whelan, "Karen Hesse Awarded MacArthur Fellowship," *School Library Journal* 48, no. 11 (November 2002): 23.

3. Whelan, "Karen Hesse Awarded MacArthur Fellowship," 23.

4. Simon & Schuster.

5. *Merriam-Webster's Collegiate Dictionary*, 10th ed., Frederic C. Mish, 486.

Chapter 1

Karen Hesse: The Person

Karen Hesse tends to be shy and reticent about her personal life, but her editor and friend, Brenda Bowen, gives us insight by telling us what she knows about Hesse:

- She's a born performer
- She's empathetic
- She makes everyone feel cherished
- She has a backbone of steel
- She loves the land
- She takes chances
- She values independence
- She has an ear for language
- She is meticulous about word choice
- She loves chocolate
- Her Jewish heritage has shaped her greatly
- She knows that death is a part of life.[1]

What has been learned about Karen Hesse while working on this manuscript:

- She's helpful
- She wants things to be correct
- She's encouraging

- She's a private person
- She cares about others
- She's proud of Randy, Kate, and Rachel and their accomplishments.

Hesse has written several autobiographical sketches for various publications, but her books tell us about her as well. When discussing her writing Hesse acknowledges drawing "on everything I have experienced thus far in life when creating story and character."[2] And in talking about her characters she says, "All of my characters, the nice ones and the not so nice ones, are splintered off my own core personality."[3] So getting to know Karen Hesse will help her readers better understand and appreciate her contributions to children's and adolescent literature.

The Early Years

On August 29, 1952, in Baltimore, Maryland, Karen made her debut into the world—two weeks early. Alvin and Frances (Broth) Donald, along with big brother Mark, welcomed the new arrival. But Karen, who had come too early and weighed only five pounds, was neither a happy nor a content baby. Hesse characterizes herself as a sickly and shy child. She talks about spending much of her childhood "bouncing from one illness to another,"[4] which made her a cranky child—a child, she thinks, who must have been very difficult. Her frequent bouts of colic could only be calmed by rides in the car; therefore, her parents spent countless hours driving around Baltimore. (Hesse says she's still addicted to car trips.) Hesse confides it is a wonder that any members of her family—nuclear or extended—continue to show any affection for her after that rocky and whiny childhood.

West Garrison Avenue

During her childhood, home was on West Garrison Avenue in the Pimlico area of Baltimore. The Donalds lived in a row house on a block with lots of children for Mark and Karen to play with, many adventures to be had, and several adult neighbors who made enough of an impression on Karen to end up as parts of characters in her books. She loved all the hustle and bustle, and at times wonders if she did her daughters a disservice by rearing them in the quiet environment of Williamsville,

Vermont. How could their childhoods have possibly been as exciting as her own?

Karen loved all of the goings-on in her community but preferred to be an observer rather than a participant. In talking about West Garrison Avenue, Hesse lists all of the children on the street. From Bonnie and Janet at one end of the block, to Cookie in the middle, and then Lois and Joey at the other end, each house held children. Some yards were bigger than others, and the more spacious areas would be where the children gathered to play games such as swinging statues and SPUD. Some yards had bigger and better toys, so the group would move on to other enticing areas.

Along with alluring yards and interesting toys, the neighborhood contained an interesting assortment of people. From the really cute guy Hesse calls "a serious 1950s male babe," to the girl who could tell the biggest whoppers, or to Joey, who had a hearing impairment, the children on West Garrison Avenue were an eclectic group. The mothers and fathers—and sometimes grandparents—were just as diverse as the children. There was Bubbe Hannah, who was Karen's babysitter any time she had to come home from school sick. The name Hannah is used by Hesse in many of her books as a tribute to this wonderful lady. But there was also the strange neighbor whom Karen and her friends feared. The children in this house weren't allowed to join the others to play; they didn't attend public school, and they weren't allowed to leave their house.

As well as the children's visiting back and forth and playing in the yards, there were neighborhood cookouts on West Garrison Avenue. But Karen never really liked these get-togethers. She says large gatherings were never something she enjoyed except for being able to watch the people. Even today as an adult, Hesse prefers small groups rather than large crowds.

Hesse describes herself as a shy child. Yet some of the stories she tells about her childhood sound very adventurous. Karen just knew that she could fly, and the row house on West Garrison Avenue is where she tried. Her first attempt was down the steps—twelve of them—from the second floor of the rowhouse, and according to her way of thinking she succeeded. She made it over the first eleven but had a rough landing—on her bottom—on the last one. There was pain, but the knowledge that she had flown made up for it. Her friend Stuart Barry Decklebaum disagreed that what she had done was flying, so Karen decided to prove that she could indeed fly. Her second attempt at flying needed to be a longer flight and, of course, from a more appropriate height. Her second-floor bedroom window seemed to be the ideal launching point. But this second attempt at flying was foiled by a neighbor. When Mrs.

Decklebaum, Stuart's mom, saw legs dangling from Karen's bedroom window, she immediately called Mrs. Donald. The preflight preparations gave Mrs. Donald enough time to race upstairs to Karen's bedroom and abort the "takeoff." (In an interview with Leonard Marcus after the publication of *Witness*, Hesse told him that she really did believe that she had flown that day down the steps.)

Another adventure combining Stuart with mischief dealt with Karen's best toy—a plastic swimming pool. Plastic wading pools can very quickly get all types of scum and mold in them; therefore, Mrs. Donald decided to give the pool a good scrubbing. When a telephone call interrupted her work, Karen and Stuart thought they would be helpful and do the scrubbing for her mom. Two children, a box of soap, and water are trouble in the making. They put the entire box of soap in the pool, turned on the hose, and watched as bubbles—lots of bubbles—began to fill the pool. All thoughts of cleaning were quickly forgotten as the pool and yard filled up with bubbles.

When Mrs. Donald returned to the yard, she quickly turned off the water, but the bubbles continued to mount. Hesse finishes this story by telling that her mother tried to grab Karen and Stuart, but that they were too slippery. When she did manage to catch one of them, the distraught mom couldn't keep hold. Karen and Stuart thought this game was fun—racing around the yard and giggling, but Mrs. Donald wasn't quite as entertained.

Parents

As Hesse so aptly puts it, her father, Alvin Donald, was a "collection man." He worked for a businessman who sold furniture and appliances. Some of the customers were less than well-off and paid their debts a few dollars a week. Mr. Donald's job was to drive to their homes and collect these payments. At times Karen made the rounds with her father, and his work and the way he treated these people made an impression on Hesse. She uses her memories of these days spent with her father in some of her stories.

Mr. Donald was also the cantor for Temple Emmanuel. Other people loved hearing his voice, but it terrified Karen. However his music brought to the house something Karen dearly loved—a piano. She enjoyed pecking out songs and entertained herself for hours with this wonderful instrument. Piano lessons lasted only about three weeks because Karen was so upset by her teacher, but her love for music has remained. Today she plays keyboard and soprano and alto recorders. In response to what she might do if she weren't a writer, Hesse says she'd love to be a conductor. "If I could start all over again, I would become a musician."[5]

Mrs. Donald began working as a substitute teacher when Karen started kindergarten. The days that she substituted in Karen's class were happy days for the child. Hesse says having her mother as the teacher made her "feel important." After Karen began first grade Mrs. Donald started working full time as a receptionist at a beauty parlor. Karen says the beauticians loved her because her "curly hair made them itchy to play."[6]

Karen greatly admired her mother. Being shy and loving to watch people, Karen admired the way her mother looked and acted. Hesse says her mother always had a presence about her when entering a room. She describes her mother as being elegant. "I loved watching her dress, loved watching her put on makeup, her perfume, brush her hair. I never had much interest myself in dressing up, but how I loved watching my mother."[7]

Karen loved her parents, but at least some of the stress in her childhood came from the fact that the couple was not suited for each other. Their conflicts seem to be an underlying reason for some of Hesse's shyness. Typical of children from homes with dissension, Karen tried to be the perfect daughter. At one point during an illness of her mother's, which she says "seemed connected to her unhappiness with my father,"[8] Karen's and her mother's roles became reversed. In an autobiographical story "Waiting for Midnight," Hesse says,

"Her doctor instructed me to take care of her: Do nothing to upset her; say nothing to upset her.

Each morning before I left for school, and each afternoon when I returned home, I would scramble eggs for my mother. I learned to make them moist, the way she liked them. From the time I left until the time I returned, and all through the evening and the long nights, my mother ate only those eggs. As I stood over the frying pan twice a day, I'd try to think good things, healing things, hoping those thoughts would enter the eggs and make my mother better."[9]

The Donalds eventually divorced, and each subsequently remarried. When Hesse talks of this extended family on both sides, she speaks fondly of everyone. *Sable* is "For Dad," and the soon-to-be-in-print *The Cats in Krasinski Square* is "In memory of my mother, Fran Levin."

Grandparents

Karen's maternal grandparents, with whom she spent a lot of time, played an important role in her childhood. She says one of her earliest memories is watching her grandfather pray in his "talis (prayer shawl) and tefillen (small leather cases worn on the head and arms)."[10] Karen would watch this early morning ritual from upstairs while he prayed downstairs; other times she'd sit on his lap as he read the *Jewish Times*. Karen and her grandmother sat together in the balcony of the orthodox synagogue where her grandmother led the Hadasseh women while the men prayed below. She and her grandmother also went shopping and out to lunch. And like many little girls, Karen loved going through her grandmother's jewelry box and touching all the pretty things collected there. Memories of grandmothers usually include food, and Karen is no exception. She remembers the silver meat grinder where her grandmother would tenderize liver.

Of her grandfather she says she remembers his gentleness—the way he dealt with people and the way he taught her "to believe in all that is good in the world."[11] Both of her grandparents have been a huge influence on her life. Since her parents weren't overly religious, Karen received her knowledge and beliefs about Judaism from these kind people.

Mark

Other happy memories of Hesse's childhood revolve around her big brother, Mark. He seems to have been the fairy tale older brother. Hesse talks about the many weekend afternoons she and Mark spent at the movies. Going to the movies was one way of releasing her mind from her always painful body, a way to forget about the ailments for a short time. (As with the car trips, Hesse still likes to take in a Sunday matinee whenever possible.) Sickly or not, one of Karen's favorite activities as a child was jumping on trampolines. This seemed to have been a fad in Baltimore in the late 1950s when Karen was young. The city had trampolines in various locations around the city, and children could jump to their heart's content—after waiting in line. The jumping was fun for Karen, but the walk home was always torture. Her sickly nature robbed her of stamina; therefore, she could walk only a short way before having to sit down and rest. Mark was always patient with her, suggesting that she take time to rest and waiting calmly for her to regain her strength. He willingly repeated this same scenario week after week when Karen would beg to be taken back to the trampolines.

Another instance where sickly, shy Hesse seems out of character is the time she decided to see just how loyal, patient, and loving Mark would be. This became known as the "spider incident." Hesse assures her readers that she is not and has never been afraid of spiders. But knowing lots of girls who were afraid gave her a frame of reference for one of her better performances. She says that one afternoon as she and Mark were doing homework in their respective bedrooms, a tiny spider began crawling across the floor in her room. With cunning in her heart, she climbed on a chair, adopted the pose of fright, and gave a blood-curdling scream. Of course, just as she had hoped, Mark quickly appeared at her doorway to save his sister from whatever danger was afoot. In response to his query as to what major catastrophe could elicit such terror, Karen pointed her trembling hand at the spider. Mark was not impressed with the spider or Karen's dilemma and quickly returned to his room and his studies. It didn't matter that he left the spider alive, the task of killing the spider unfinished. What mattered was that Karen had received the response she wanted (and needed) from her big brother. Mark, like all true fairy tale heroes, could be counted on in a life-or-death situation.

Mark and Karen had a common love for animals. Kitty-Tiger, a stray cat the siblings convinced their parents to let them keep, is still fondly remembered. They loved that cat and spent countless hours playing with it. Kitty-Tiger mysteriously disappeared, and after several days of searching, Mark and Karen willingly believed a story that a boy from the next block had thrown Kitty-Tiger off a cliff. This tragedy took away Mark's desire for other pets, but Karen was delighted when a friend of the family (later to become her stepfather) brought Snooper, a beagle puppy, to their home. Later the family moved from the row house to an apartment that didn't accept pets. It broke Karen's heart but Snooper had to be given away. This trauma of losing yet another beloved pet helped Karen—like Mark—"swear off" pets until years later when Noe and Kiku, two more cats, came into the picture. Patty and Pippi, two cats, and Sasha, a dog who thought she was a cat, were later family pets, but as Hesse so aptly puts it, "have moved on to another plane." (When Hesse and husband Randy traveled the country for six months early in their married life, their traveling companions were Noe and Kiku.)

Summer Camp

As soon as Karen was old enough she attended sleepover summer camps. She's sure her parents allowed this to insure their own sanity. (Hesse says that when she was a child, her mother hung a calendar on her wall, and each day that Karen didn't cry, she'd get a gold star. Unfortunately for Karen and the entire family, those gold stars usually stayed in the box rather than getting put on the calendar!) Since her whining and crankiness was a constant in their lives, everyone needed and enjoyed the time apart. But Karen liked the camp. She loved the discipline, structure, and routine that camp afforded her. Her favorite sport was archery, and surprisingly, she was very good. This is another example of sickly Karen's not fitting the mold. To pull the strings on a bow takes a great deal of strength, yet Karen became very accomplished at this sport and even taught archery as a counselor at another camp.

But most of all she loved the chocolate pudding. Since it was purchased in huge quantities, already prepared, this concoction made the perfect dessert to serve the campers. It seems that some of her fellow campers were not as fond of the delicacy as Karen, so they willingly shared their portions with her. Hesse says she ate the pudding until she made herself sick. But as soon as her stomach settled down—about the time chocolate pudding was again served—she was back eating all she could get her hands on. Karen was fifteen but going into her senior year in high school when she was told about a job at another camp. It was very convenient to let the camp officials assume she was seventeen or eighteen and she got the job. Being a counselor was not quite as enjoyable as being a camper, but she survived the summer.

Summer camp is another place where quiet, shy Karen seems to have shown a different face. Hesse, who says she thrives on rules and regulations, for some reason decided to show her "stubborn streak" and refused (Hesse says she "defiantly" refused) to do a task assigned to her. This action sent her to the dreaded Miss Ida, the disciplinarian. The consequences of Karen's actions weren't as bad as they could have been, but she learned her lesson and didn't have to "go before" Miss Ida again.

Being by Herself

But life was not always this lively for Karen. Hesse talks about not having an easy childhood. In her words, "It had a lot of bumps. I'm not certain when I realized I wasn't like my friends. But from an early age it felt right to keep my inner world a secret."[12] Hesse remembers being more of an observer of life rather than an active participant. She confesses "[I] spent much of my time as a little recorder of life, taking things in without entirely participating in them."[13] Karen spent many hours alone in her bedroom writing poetry, sitting in the apple tree in the backyard reading, or visiting the Enoch Pratt Free Library with its wonderful books and librarian.

The way Karen best expressed herself during her childhood was through writing. She poured her heart out onto pages of notebook paper. Her bedroom was quite small and confining, so when she finished her writing, she'd go to the apple tree and read or watch the goings-on of the neighborhood. The alley she could see from her perch in the tree held wondrous sights of people and animals going about all sorts of business. The tree was not the most comfortable place, but it afforded Karen the privacy she wanted. So even though her bony bottom would go numb, she continued to ignore and endure the discomfort.

Enoch Pratt Free Library

The Enoch Pratt Free Library was another safe haven for Hesse. It gave her the books she so loved to read, but the library also gave her Peggy Coughlin—the librarian. Losing herself in books was another way for Karen to get out of her sickly body. Ms. Coughlin was a lifesaver by suggesting appropriate books for her to read. Karen read through Dr. Seuss and the picture books, children's chapter books, and finally arrived at the novels—all the time being guided through her selections by Peggy Coughlin. Hesse says from *Horton Hatches the Egg* to John Hersey's *Hiroshima*, she learned lessons in survival. From Horton she "learned about honor, dedication, and loyalty. Horton became her model for what it means to be a humanitarian."[14] Reading *Hiroshima* at the age of twelve led to what she refers to as the end of her childhood. Being exposed to war and all its ramifications showed her that people can, and do, survive no matter the circumstances. Of *Hiroshima* she says, "The courage, the profound compassion, dignity, and humanity of the Japanese people in the face of such unfathomable destruction helped me see the world in a way I never had before. When I closed the covers of *Hiroshima*, I closed the door on my childhood. The impact of Hersey's book is apparent when you read my story set in the aftermath of an accident at a nuclear power plant, *Phoenix Rising*."[15]

Elementary School

Ms. Coughlin aided Karen's love for reading, but her love for writing was nurtured during her elementary years at P.S. 223 (or Pimlico Elementary School) when two teachers—Mrs. Datnoff and Mr. Ball—encouraged Karen's creative endeavors. Being a shy child, she discovered that writing fiction created a sense of power that helped overcome her fears. She says,

> At night I would fantasize that I was an ambassador between Khrushchev and Kennedy. . . . I would be the person who would save the world because I would make these two people understand each other and resolve their differences . . . that's when I discovered the power of fiction because it was very comforting for me to feel as if I had some control and I could do something, and that's what creating fiction is all about.[16]

Karen loved kindergarten and her early years in school, but it was Mrs. Datnoff, her fifth-grade teacher, who jump-started her writing. Mrs. Datnoff assigned a short story as a writing assignment for the students. Hesse wrote a fantasy story about a bubble world. When the paper was returned, Mrs. Datnoff had given Karen a big check plus and written "very creative" on the paper. Hesse says she was the type of child who was not accustomed to receiving a lot of positive reinforcement; this recognition from Mrs. Datnoff was like a gift. Because her teacher believed in Karen's writing and creative ability, Karen believed in it, too. Hesse says that throughout the years with all of the rejections her writings have received, she has continued to play the tape in her mind of what Mrs. Datnoff had written on her paper in the fifth grade.

Whether Mrs. Datnoff confided or shared her opinion of Karen's writing with Mr. Ball, the sixth-grade teacher, isn't known, but Mr. Ball also saw her potential as a writer. Hesse refers to Mr. Ball as an "extraordinary" teacher. She says her shyness was at an all-time high and that she couldn't even look anyone in the face. But when Mr. Ball asked Karen to write the sixth-grade graduation speech, she was delighted to accommodate him. After all, Mrs. Datnoff had convinced her that she could write and was very creative, so Mr. Ball's request confirmed what Karen already believed about herself—she was a writer.

But Mr. Ball had another surprise for Karen. After she had written the speech and he had read it, Mr. Ball asked her to give the speech at the graduation ceremony. Did he have in mind for Karen to read the speech all along or was the speech so good that he decided the author should get the credit by giving it herself? We don't know the answer. But we do know that Karen said "yes" to his request and read the speech. Graduation was a standing-room-only crowd, and Hesse remembers that she delivered the speech with "amazing polish for a backward, tongue-tied 11-year-old."[17]

Hesse, in retelling this episode in her life, says that everyone—herself included—was surprised by her abilities. The only person who wasn't in the least surprised was Mr. Ball. But Hesse thinks this was an eye-opener for her mother and that this might have been the first time that her mother truly saw her as a person of talent and ability. Hesse talks about, as a child, fading into the background so that she could go unnoticed, which she greatly preferred, not always giving people the opportunity to realize or recognize her talents.

High School

High school brought new challenges and experiences for Hesse. During this period of time her parents, who had not had the best of relationships for several years, divorced. They each subsequently remarried, and Karen moved from West Garrison Avenue to Baltimore County—from being a city girl to living in a suburban setting. The row house was exchanged for an apartment that didn't accept pets, so she had to give away her beloved Snooper. And even though the row houses were close together, living in an apartment setting left less room for privacy and made the family even more conscious of any disturbances they might create.

Another change for Karen was gaining a new family. After both parents remarried, Karen acquired another brother and two sisters. In an autobiographical sketch Hesse mentions her stepsister, Randy, but adds "it's been a long time since I thought of her as anything but a full sister."[18] And in my correspondence with Hesse, she has stressed that her siblings are just that, with no hyphenated designations. "I do not refer to them as step and biological. They are all my siblings: Mark, Randy, Joyce, and Barry."[19]

In high school Hesse discovered a different outlet for her creative side. Thanks to her new sister, Randy, and a high school drama teacher, Karen became enamored of the theater. Randy was a dancer—a very good dancer. While still in high school she danced professionally, and shy Karen was a bit envious of all the attention Randy got because of her talent and looks. Not only was Randy an excellent dancer, but also exotic and beautiful. Hesse's description of herself is much less flattering. "I often looked, and still look like a refugee."[20]

At Pikesville High School Karen enrolled in an acting class. The drama teacher was Joan Maruskin, and she, like Mrs. Datnoff and Mr. Ball, had a great influence on Hesse. Ms. Maruskin was a no-nonsense type of teacher who believed in hard work and following the rules—her rules—when it came to the drama classes. For Karen, who had thrived on the structure and rules of summer camp, this relationship proved to be the perfect match. Karen loved the teacher, the class, and whatever task was set before her. Karen loved being on stage because she could be someone else. Hesse talks about losing herself in the characters she played even to the point of forgetting that she was on stage. She says, "Suddenly I sort of 'woke up' and noticed people were crying. I had no idea really what I'd said or done, but whatever it was seemed to have an extraordinary effect on people."[21] Acting was yet another way for Karen to get out of her own body.

All of this drama training may have had a bearing on one of Hesse's most unusual performances. At the senior variety show where it was typical to make a fool of oneself on stage, Karen decided to join in. For the shy, serious Karen this decision was quite a breakthrough. She says that no one ever expected her to participate in something like this. As a matter of fact, most people thought she didn't know how to have fun. But the joke was definitely on them. Mrs. Donald taught Karen a silly song about ship-builder blues and bananas and created a costume that Hesse says made her look like "a sixteen-year-old Chiquita Banana lady!"[22] The song, costume, and Karen's delivery were all a huge success. The audience thoroughly appreciated the performance. The cheering continued through ten bows. Hesse says that these accolades might be the moment when her sense of humor was born.

College

After the wonderful experiences on the stage, Karen decided that she would like to major in drama in college. But college admissions became a hurdle that she would have to overcome. Due to family turmoil, Karen's academics had suffered during her sophomore year in high school—she had failed both math and French. Making good, solid grades in her junior and senior years couldn't overcome the deficit created previously. This dilemma caused Ms. Maruskin to step in again to help Karen.

Knowing that Karen was looking toward theater as a profession, Ms. Maruskin took her to Towson State College (now University) in Towson, Maryland, and introduced her to people in the theater department. Ms. Maruskin also made phone calls and wrote letters, and Karen was, in her own words—"wonder of wonders"—accepted at Towson. She spent two semesters at Towson but, as her readers know, didn't become an actress. She explains her change of career goals in two words: Randy Hesse.

Being a theater major meant doing lots of jobs besides simply acting on stage. One of her responsibilities was to run lights for some of the student productions. As Karen was working in the light booth getting ready for a production, a young man she didn't know came up. A friend introduced Karen Donald to Randy Hesse, and Karen says it was love at first sight. Falling in love made her realize that a career in the theater was not going to be possible—that she couldn't possibly do both. Love and the theater both were full-time commitments, so she chose Randy Hesse and has never regretted it.

After that first year at Towson State, Karen transferred to the University of Maryland at College Park. During the Thanksgiving break of 1971 Randy and Karen eloped because Randy got his orders to go overseas with the Navy. (Their respective families were not too thrilled with the romance. Hesse says they would have tried harder for family approval had Randy not received his orders.) They moved to Norfolk, Virginia, for two years. Randy sailed the seas on his battleship, and Karen became one of the "wives who wait."

When Randy's tour of duty was over, they returned to College Park to complete their degrees. The date of Hesse's graduation from the University of Maryland seems to be a mystery. In response to the question of when she graduated, Hesse replied that she thought she graduated in the fall of 1975, but an article about her that appeared in the University of Maryland *Terp* gave her graduation date as 1974. All parties do agree that she graduated with a bachelor's degree in English with double minors in psychology and anthropology.

The poetry that Hesse began writing in her small room in the row house on West Garrison Avenue flourished while she was in college. During her years at the University of Maryland, Hesse was frequently asked to read her work there and at other universities in the area. Also, several of her poems appeared in the university's literary magazine, but a full collection of these works was never published. Perhaps her readers may at some point have an opportunity to read these poems. Hesse says the poems are in a file cabinet in her office, and "my daughter Kate is in the process of organizing me."

Adult Years

After their graduations and to celebrate the Bicentennial, for six months in 1976 Karen and Randy, accompanied by their two cats, tent camped while traveling across America. They put shelves in their pickup truck, added a Coleman lantern, stove, and a few clothes and "took off." While on this journey they visited most of the National Parks, met people, and fell in love with the land—ending their travels in Brattleboro, Vermont. Hesse says, "I knew as soon as we crossed the Connecticut River from New Hampshire into Vermont that I'd come home. I found work, joined a writing group, gave birth to two children, and learned how to survive endless weeks of sub-zero temperature and great tunnels of dazzling snow."[23]

Those great tunnels of dazzling snow and the harsh winters of Vermont were not as enticing to Hesse after several years. In an interview with Leonard Marcus, she confesses that there was a time when she thought about leaving the cold winters, but after visiting numerous places nothing was quite as appealing. Vermont is not only beautiful, but the people there are also exceptional. Hesse says that Vermonters are known for their tolerance of differing lifestyles, points of view, religious persuasions—of anything and everything. For someone who writes about prejudices in all of her stories, the atmosphere of tolerance must be a breath of fresh air.

In 1979 Kate was born, and Rachel joined the family in 1982. Karen Hesse is extremely proud of her daughters. Both Kate and Rachel were born at home. Hesse writes that Rachel was born around midnight, and the next morning she was up doing laundry, carrying Rachel around like a football. At the time of this writing, both young women are in their twenties and still studying. Kate tried law school, but decided it wasn't for her. She is now enrolled in art classes. Rachel is at a university in Montreal. Like her mom, Rachel is interested in archaeology. Neither Kate nor Rachel is currently looking at writing as a career. That choice could always change. Hesse says Rachel "has a remarkable ear for 'voice,' but her interests are so diverse it would be unfair to pin her down just yet."[24] Many of Hesse's books are dedicated to Randy, Kate, and Rachel, but *Just Juice* is "For Kate . . . just Kate" and *Stowaway* is "To Rachel, whose future I cannot endeavor to imagine."

Hesse's husband Randy modestly calls himself a carpenter, but Hesse says, "If you ask me, I'd say he's a furniture maker. He makes beautiful furniture and cabinetry, but he's replaced too many rotted sills over the course of his career to think of himself as anything but a carpenter."[25]

For years, the Hesses made their home in Williamsville, Vermont. After many years of writing at home, getting up at three or four o'clock in the morning when an idea would hit or writing late into the night, Hesse decided to move her writing to an office/apartment in Brattleboro. Late nights or early mornings now didn't disturb family members, and this arrangement gave her space to create while looking at either the Wantastiquet Mountains of New Hampshire or the Connecticut River. In 1998 Hesse gave up "that sweet little apartment" when she and Randy sold the house in Williamsville and bought an 1880 Queen Anne house in Brattleboro.

We recognize Hesse as an outstanding writer of literature for children and young adults, but her neighbors know her as a community servant. She's served on a local school board as well as a board of the public library. Hesse has also been the leader for the Southern Vermont Chapter of the Society of Children's Book Writers and Illustrators. She is affiliated with the hospice movement in her area. (In response to a query about this involvement, Hesse said she learned about hospice when their volunteers assisted her grandmother to "a dignified death. I wanted to give something back to this wonderful organization.")[26] For several years, the Hesse family hosted foreign exchange students for the summer. The students came from all over the world: Europe, Asia, and South America. Karen Hesse doesn't just write about making the world a better place, she and her family work toward this end in their daily lives.

Notes

1. Brenda Bowen, "Karen Hesse," *Horn Book Magazine* 74, no. 4. (July/August 1998): 428–432.

2. Judy O'Malley, "Talking with . . . Karen Hesse," Book Links 9 no. 1 (September 1999): 55.

3. Judy O'Malley, "Talking with . . . Karen Hesse," 55.

4. Alan Hedblad, ed., "Karen Hesse," in *Something about the Author* 113. (Farmington, MI: Gale Group, 2000), 67.

5. *Something about the Author*, "Karen Hesse," 82.

6. *Something about the Author*, "Karen Hesse," 67.

7. *Something about the Author*, "Karen Hesse," 67.

8. Karen Hesse, "Waiting for Midnight," *When I Was Your Age: Original Stories about Growing Up* 2nd ed. Amy Ehrlich (Cambridge, MA: Candlewick Press, 2002), 155.

9. Karen Hesse, "Waiting for Midnight," 155.

10. *Something about the Author*, "Karen Hesse," 69.

11. *Something about the Author*, "Karen Hesse," 69.

12. "Karen Hesse," *Eighth Book of Junior Authors and Illustrators*, ed. Connie C. Rockman. (NY: H.W. Wilson Company, 2000), 216.

13. Alan Hedblad, ed., "Karen Hesse," in *Something about the Author* 103. (Farmington, MI: Gale Group, 1999), 80.

14. Lois T. Stover, "Karen Hesse," *Writers for Young Adults*, ed. Ted Hipple (NY: Charles Schribners and Sons, 2000), 93–101.

15. *Something about the Author*, "Karen Hesse," 77–78.

16. Cathy Beck, Linda Gwyn, Dick Koblitz, Anne O'Connor, Kathryn Mitchell Pierce, and Susan Wolf, "Talking About Books: Karen Hesse," *Language Arts* 76 (January 1999): 263.

17. Karen Hesse, "Unforgettable Teachers: Thank You, Mr. Ball," *Instructor (Primary Edition)* 108, no. 5 (January/February 1999): 87.

18. *Something about the Author*, "Karen Hesse," 75.

19. Personal email correspondence with Karen Hesse.

20. *Something about the Author*, "Karen Hesse," 75.

21. *Something about the Author*, "Karen Hesse," 75.

22. *Something about the Author*, "Karen Hesse," 80.

23. "Karen Hesse," *Educational Paperback Association* 2001, www.edupaperback.org/authorbios/Hesse_Karen.html (12 September 2001).

24. Email correspondence.

25. Email correspondence.

26. Email correspondence.

Chapter 2

Writing for Children and Young Adults

How It All Began

As a child on West Garrison Avenue, Hesse dreamed of numerous occupations such as archeologist, ambassador, actor, and author. These dreams were fostered by her varied childhood experiences, the books she read from the Enoch Pratt Free Library, and encouragement from several teachers. In the process of becoming the author we know her to be today, she tried many different jobs. Hesse says she's earned wages as a waitress (making pizza bagels), nanny (she worked such long hours she ended up with mononucleosis), library worker (as a student work study job in college), personnel officer, agricultural laborer, advertising secretary, typesetter, proofreader, mental health care provider, substitute teacher, and book reviewer. Many of these jobs were to help support herself during college, but some she did while being a full-time mom and an aspiring writer. After her stint in the library at the University of Maryland, which she loved, this energetic lady has tried to make sure that her jobs related in some way to reading. Like many other authors, Hesse took a circuitous route to the profession. Though rejections came from her first attempts at being published, she wouldn't give up this dream.

A Little Help from the Family

As noted earlier, Karen Hesse's first professional literary endeavor was as a poet when she was in college. She continued writing poetry until after she became pregnant with Kate. Hesse says the total dedication of mind that she needed for creating poetry was not compatible with motherhood. Caring for Kate—and later Rachel—took away the time and quiet needed for the focus and concentration required for writing this genre. In her Newbery acceptance speech Hesse so eloquently says that for seventeen years poetry was put on hold because "my ability to focus on the creation of poetry diminished as my need to focus on the creation of human life increased."[1] These two wonderful daughters Hesse helped create are one of the reasons she's writing for children and young adult readers today. While the girls were growing up, mother and daughters regularly visited the children's section of the library for read-aloud books. Hesse says, "When I began reading children's literature to my daughters, I felt I'd discovered at last the key to releasing my secret inner world."[2] When *Wish on a Unicorn* was published, she says it felt like "a lifetime of bottling up my imagination ended."[3]

Reading to her daughters as well as having worked as a typesetter, proofreader, and book reviewer had exposed Hesse to a wide range of books. Some of these works struck her as being very unsatisfying. Having considered herself a writer since fifth grade when Mrs. Datnoff wrote those words "very creative" on her story, Hesse thought she could write "at least as well if not better"[4] than some of the books she and her daughters were finding in the library or some she had read while typesetting, proofreading, or reviewing.

It was during her visits to the library with Kate and Rachel that she discovered the works of Katherine Paterson. In an interview with Lois Stover, Hesse says she stumbled across *Of Nightingales That Weep* and fell in love with Paterson's writing. She remembers thinking to herself, "If this is children's literature, then I want to be a part of it!"[5] Hesse began to immerse herself in children's literature in 1981 and then started to market her own work in 1985. Her first attempt as a children's author was the story of a family's encounter with Bigfoot. The editor (the above mentioned Brenda Bowen) who read this manuscript said the story wasn't credible, but the "voice was something to remember. I thought: 'This is a writer.'"[6] Bowen recognized Hesse's talent and was intrigued by the return address—Star Route. So when a second manuscript arrived from this address, Bowen was delighted, and in

1991 *Wish on a Unicorn* was published.

In 1992 *Letters from Rifka* was published, and this book gave Hesse her first national recognition. *Letters from Rifka* was named the International Reading Association's Book of the Year. Of course, Hesse was invited to come to an IRA conference to accept her award. Receiving the award was wonderful, but she was especially delighted to learn that the keynote speaker for this occasion was none other than Katherine Paterson. Hesse and Paterson were seated next to each other at the head table, which gave Hesse an outstanding opportunity to confide her admiration for Paterson's work. Paterson was delighted to know that she had played a role in the development of another children's writer. They began a professional relationship that has turned into a personal friendship.

It wasn't just her immediate family who helped Karen Hesse become a writer. In her Newbery acceptance speech she says, "There are so many to thank. My zayde, who sold his ticket on the *Titanic* and took the next boat over; my bubbe, Sara; my mom, Fran; my aunts, Esther and Bernice; my whole delicious family."[7] This "whole delicious family" along with friends, acquaintances, and sometimes strangers has contributed to her stories—sometimes by their traits being used in characters, sometimes with story ideas, and sometimes with moral support.

Family Is Important

Hesse's books explore all types of families—nuclear, extended, and community. In an interview in *BookLinks* Hesse talks about family in her stories. She says, "Family does figure prominently in my work. Not necessarily conventional family, but family created when people take responsibility for their neighbors, when they care for and are cared for by one another."[8] Hesse gives us her definition of family in *The Music of Dolphins* when Mila asks Sandy what a family is. Sandy replies: "Family is people you love and care for, people who love and care for you."[9] Hesse says that her family, neighbors, teachers, and community all helped in taking care of her, and she adds another dimension: "And beyond them (my family), my literary family, books, characters, kept me afloat during the times I was too tired to keep dog-paddling in the rapids of my life."[10] She continues by adding, "If a child can find a community of support, what a difference that community can make. It doesn't take much. A single book, a single understanding word, a single act of kindness can sustain a child through dozens of hard knocks."[11] The single book to which she is referring could be one of hers. Readers could easily put themselves in the place of Billie Jo, Rifka, Hannah, Leanora, Nicholas, et al., and learn lessons in coping and adapting to any situation or experience.

Readers Are Important

The insight Hesse has for her readers is phenomenal. She thinks that children are "thoughtful, smart, funny, generous, compassionate, kind, and wise."[12] Hesse realizes that her readers are asking for substance in their reading and for authors who show them respect; therefore, she writes about complex issues on subjects as varied as ecology, history, prejudices, and family. These young adult readers are looking for books that challenge their intelligence, confirm their beliefs, and console them in their times of turmoil. Hesse believes that young readers want adults to listen to their questions and help them find the answers. She also wants her writings to uplift, inform, and entertain her readers. Because Hesse believes the best legacy we can give the younger generation is to value reading and to love books, she writes books that the younger generation wants to read.

Hesse uplifts, informs, and entertains her readers on topics as varied as Captain James Cook's voyage to chart new lands, lighthouse-keeping during the Civil War, the 1917-1918 Spanish influenza epidemic in Boston, Europe during the First World War, the KKK in Vermont during the 1920s, the Dust Bowl in the 1930s, the Aleut relocation during World War II, the social structure of dolphins, and the effects of a nuclear meltdown. While uplifting, informing, and entertaining her readers, she also weaves in themes of family, heroines/heroes, prejudices, fear of the unknown, love, forgiveness, and the struggles associated with coming of age for her adolescent protagonists.

In a 1999 *BookLinks* interview, Judy O'Malley asked Hesse if she consciously considered the educational value of her books. Hesse's response was that she carefully researches her work because she loves to do research and wants the stories to be accurate and authentic. Of research she says, "I *love* discovering new things. I feel so fortunate that I have a job that encourages me to read and discover new things."[13] This enthusiasm for knowledge very quickly is transferred to her readers. And realizing this fact, she says, "Yes, I know that sometimes my work may be the first and perhaps the only exposure a reader will have to a period in history. I am thrilled when my books are recognized as notable in the field of social studies and when I discover another teacher using my work in the classroom."[14] But she doesn't set out to write works for the classroom. She sets out to tell a good story for her readers to enjoy: a story that will challenge their intelligence, confirm and expand their beliefs, and give consolation when it's needed—in other words uplift, inform, and entertain. With or without the classroom and a teacher, Hesse's books are an educational experience. A review of *Stowaway* in *School Library Journal* observes that her "subtle yet thorough attention to detail creates a memorable tale that is a virtual encyclopedia of life in the days when England ruled the seas."[15] It's obvious that her research and varied topics are constantly opening the eyes and minds of her readers, just as all those books from the Enoch Pratt Free Library did for her so many years ago. In her own reading she enjoys books "that have grit and make me feel like I've learned something when I've finished."[16] Hesse may be talking about the type of books she likes to read, but her readers know that she is also describing the type of books she writes.

Making the World a Better Place

Hesse's childhood fantasy of being the catalyst that brought together Kennedy and Khrushchev didn't happen, but her writing does produce positive effects for her readers. Through the characters in Hesse's books the reader discovers that they, too, can care for themselves and others as well as recognize their own potential. This sense of power she gives to readers may be her strongest asset. She says that in a way all of her work is about tragedy and hope. "Perhaps it is the universal theme of the human spirit—choosing life in spite of and because of sorrow."[17] This philosophy is what pulls her into the projects she chooses. She continues, "I am drawn to stories about regular people transcending the challenges and obstacles life places in their paths."[18] "Tikkum Olam" is a phrase in the Jewish tradition which has come to mean "to repair the world" in the sense of making it a better place to live by caring for others as well as the environment. Hesse's books fit this concept and fulfill her childhood dream of saving the world. She did not have the opportunity to make Kennedy and Khrushchev understand each other and resolve their differences, but she is using her talents to be an ambassador between young adult readers and the world.

One way to help the world become a better place is by taking care of one another. In their process of maturation, Hesse's young adult protagonists learn how to take care of themselves and then how to take care of others, their community, and the environment. Her characters are not superheroes; they are typical teenagers with the typical problems of fitting in, egocentrism, and parents. At first the protagonists learn how to take care of themselves and their own problems, and then they learn how to help take care of their families and communities. The chasm that grows between Billie Jo and Daddy in *Out of the Dust* gets bigger each day. Not until Billie Jo is able to accept that Ma's death truly was an accident can she forgive herself and her father. They can then begin to regain their loving relationship. Nyle in *Phoenix Rising* must come to terms with her terror of the "dying room" before she can help Muncie lose her fear of radiation poisoning and Ezra his fear of death. In order for Hannah (*A Time of Angels*) to take care of her sisters, she must relinquish control to Vashti. For strong, independent Hannah, having to rely on someone else is tantamount to failure, but she learns that this choice is the best.

A second way to care for the world is to produce beauty. Whether Hesse is writing in free verse poetry, diary, or narrative format, her words work together to create literature of aesthetic quality. The Newbery committee that awarded the 1998 medal to *Out of the Dust* recognized Hesse's ability to create this beauty. *Publisher's Weekly* says Hesse "turns language into music,"[19] and *Kirkus Review* says of the language in *Witness*, "What Copeland created with music, and Hopper created with paint, Hesse deftly and unerringly creates with words."[20]

Entertaining and educating an audience are yet other ways of helping to save the world. Hesse's works are definitely entertaining as is shown by the numerous awards and positive reviews she gets from both the literary critics and her readers. She educates her readers about historical, social, and environmental topics, but most importantly she educates her readers about life—their own and those of the other people with whom they might come in contact. After spending three years with the seamen of the *Endeavour* along with the natives he meets on the islands, Nicholas understands and appreciates these people who are so completely different from his gentry background in England.

Hesse manages, by writing in several genres and on various topics, to use these young people and their stories to entertain and educate the reader by sharing ways that they can take care of themselves and their world. By doing this she is continuing her quest—begun when she was a child—of saving the world.

Where Do Your Characters Come From?

Her ideas don't always come from her family, but many of the characters—at least some of their traits—can be found in family and friends. Hesse tries not to base a character directly on someone real, but she does blend characteristics and qualities of people she knows in order to create a character for her books. The problem, she says, of drawing directly on someone alive would be an invasion of his or her privacy and problematic if the character needs to do something the real person has never or would never do. But she is willing to share some of those blended characters.

The use of the name Hannah in Hesse's stories comes from Bubbe Hannah, the neighbor and surrogate grandmother to the children in the row houses on West Garrison Avenue. Hesse has named several characters Hannah, "perhaps because this dear woman played such an important role in my early years."[21] Hesse says she unconsciously began using the name Hannah whenever a character was kind, generous, and gentle spirited. A young reader named Hannah called Hesse's attention to the frequency with which she used the name. The name Vera also can be found more than once in Hesse's books, perhaps because this was her mother-in-law's name.

The personalities and some physical traits of Tante Rose and Vashti in *A Time of Angels* are modeled after the two older women who ran the summer camp Hesse attended as a child. Some of Vashti's negative traits are based on Miss Ida—the disciplinarian from Hesse's camp days. (Miss Ida also had different colored eyes—a trait Vashti shares.) *Letters from Rifka* is based on the story of her great-aunt's memories of her immigration from Russia during the post–World War I period, but Rifka's feisty and spunky personality is drawn from memories Hesse has of her friend, Mickey.

Hesse says that her grandparents are the inspiration behind *Letters from Rifka* and also the picture book *Poppy's Chair*. Her maternal grandparents' "spirit can be found in each good deed my characters perform."[22] The character Hannah in *A Time of Angels* may get her name from Bubbe Hannah, but her personality is based on Hesse's Aunt Esther. Like Hannah in *A Time of Angels* Aunt Esther was the eldest of three sisters and had the responsibility of rearing the younger girls. Hesse continues, "Hannah Gold is outspoken, bold, independent. That was my Aunt Esther, through and through."[23] Aunt Bern is the person behind the aunt in *Lavender*, and a young hearing-impaired friend from the West Garrison Avenue days, Joey, is where Hesse gets her affection for people with disabilities. She refers to them as "people who are set apart from society."[24] Several of Hesse's books include characters that are different from the norm either physically or mentally. Muncie (*Phoenix Rising*) is small of stature; Hannie (*Wish on a Unicorn*) is mentally challenged; Corey (*Lester's Dog*) is hearing impaired.

Hesse uses some of her father's personality traits in her characters. Alvin Donald was a "collection man." His job was to visit the homes of the less fortunate people and pick up their payments for various debts. At times she was allowed to ride along with her father on some of his rounds. She liked doing this because it gave her time with her father, and she saw him in a different light. One of the things that impressed Karen most about her father and his job was that he never considered these people to be lesser than he. Their homes and living conditions were not what Mr. Donald was accustomed to, yet he knew each person and would always ask about his or her day, health, and other members of the family. She also remembers the humor and dignity of these people—dignity her father helped keep intact by the way he responded to them and his job. When Hesse wrote *Wish on a Unicorn* and *Just Juice*—two of her chapter books for intermediate readers—she remembered the humor and the dignity she had seen in these people on her father's collection route. Hesse says she tried to give Mags and Juice this same dignity.

Ideas and Radios, Televisions, Libraries, and Bookstores

Even though her family and friends help with ideas and characters, Hesse uses various other sources for her stories. As an adult Hesse continues the observation of her surroundings that she began as a youngster. She says she loves to "haunt bookstores, conduct interviews, comb the shelves of public libraries, . . . study, probe, and sift."[25] She reads constantly—newspapers, magazines, books, whatever is available. She loves to listen to National Public Radio. Her infrequent television viewing is limited to documentaries. Hesse "absorbs mountains of details, most of which are quite interesting. But every now and then something totally captivates me, breaks my heart, takes my breath away. Those are the details that become my books."[26]

Hesse got the idea for *The Music of Dolphins* from listening to "Fresh Air With Terry Gross" on NPR. Gross did an interview with the author of a book about an adolescent girl who had lived in an environment where she used no language. When she was taken out of this environment, the girl was placed in a hospital setting where speech pathologists began working with her. Hesse was intrigued by the story, but more concerned for the young woman who had been "abused all her life by her parents, and then she was handed over to the scientific community and exploited by them."[27] Hesse decided that she needed to write a story about feral children, so she began doing research and talking with speech pathologists. Jill, a friend from Hesse's college days, is a speech therapist, so she and another friend became consultants for how Mila's language development would have worked. Emotionally this was one of the hardest books for Hesse to write because of the vulnerability of Mila, the main character. Hesse says that she probably did more research for *The Music of Dolphins* and *Just Juice* than any of her others. For *The Music of Dolphins* Hesse researched language development. Not only did she research language development, but she also spent time in Florida researching dolphins and their social order. For *Just Juice* she had to delve into the problems associated with reading difficulties.

The idea for *Witness* came from an airline magazine. To fill in the last few minutes of a flight, Hesse picked up the magazine and began to thumb through, glancing at the articles. She noticed a short piece on the KKK in Vermont in the 1920s. Thinking this article had to be a mistake—surely the KKK had never been that far north—Hesse decided to research the topic. As she found out from old newspapers and other archives, the Klan had indeed tried to make its presence known in Vermont. Realizing that if she didn't know of this existence, then others didn't either, she decided to tell the story.

Randomness

Hesse does love to research, but she says sometimes the randomness of life adds to her books. It could be a book she's reading for pleasure at the time, a concert or lecture she attends, or something that happens at home. But this randomness could be the reason for some of the twists and turns that her stories take. In her first draft writing stage when there's the "stream of consciousness," these other elements in her life may have a way of filtering into the story.

Characters Run the Show

Hesse explains that her work is very much character driven; therefore, she begins with the voice of the narrator. "I can hear the character speaking, I can hear the cadence of the voice and that voice draws action, action draws the plot to it."[28] Once she hears the voice of her character, she writes very quickly—sometimes working day and night ("I'm compulsive.")—until she has a spare draft of thirty to sixty pages. This writing seems to be stream of consciousness, and Hesse is unaware of what she's written. It is at this point that she reads what has been written "because I haven't a clue what the book is about, why the book is about that, or what the character's motivation is, what the character needs."[29] In this first draft she is listening to the character's voice and puts that voice in context of the research that has been done. Also during this first draft Hesse goes into what she refers to as a channel of energy. This phase puts her where she can "smell, touch, taste, or hear the elements of the story."[30]

Since her stories are so character driven and she works from listening to the voice of the narrator, Hesse was asked about the challenge of shifting from one voice to another as she writes. She responded that it wasn't really that difficult for her since each voice is so unique. And she uses picture boards, so that makes shifting voices easier. Moving from voice to voice within a story is different from moving from one story to another. She says it can take as long as a week for her to change story voices. (This happens when she has multiple projects—working on one while another may be with the editor.)

In an interview with Leonard Marcus, Hesse talks about how she created characters and their personalities for *Witness*. Hesse said she had each character begin as an animal. She then used that animal's characteristics for those of the person. An example she gives is Harvey Pettibone. Viola refers to him as a "mule." His character is stubborn, hardheaded, and slow to change. By using these animal qualities Hesse reiterates her love for used bookstores. From these places she gets many unique books—once discovering a book on the "symbolism of animals, flowers, trees." While creating characters for *Witness*, she used this book which she randomly picked off her shelves. (This could be some of the previously mentioned randomness!)

Hesse loves to name her characters. As mentioned previously some of the characters are named for people who have a special significance to Hesse. The other names don't simply drop out of the sky. She works very hard at naming her characters so that they fit into the time period as well as having their names fit their personalities. From those wonderful bookstores she loves so well, Hesse has collected a shelf full of books about naming babies. These books are organized in several ways. Some are by generation; some are ethnic; some are by gender—many different ways. When Hesse is choosing names for her characters, she looks for how the name sounds in the reader's head—how pronounceable the name is, the meaning of the name, the ethnic background, how strong the name is—what it suggests to the reader. She says every name goes through a checklist before it's used, and still sometimes the names get changed during the writing process.

Timeline for Writing

This first draft is usually finished within a couple of weeks and then the revisions begin. Her stories are told through the voice of a narrator—usually the main character. Knowing her audience, she realizes that readers respond best to first-person narration. In her writing she says that she can hear the character speaking, hear the cadence of the voice. She often uses pictures to help her "hear" the voice of the narrator. A picture board or a single picture is placed so that it can be seen while she is writing. She looks into the eyes of these photographs and asks, "Would you do this? Would you say this? Would you act this way?"[31] These are pictures of real people who lived during the time period that the story is set. Hesse collects books and albums of pictures from used bookstores and uses these as well as albums of friends when looking for the exact character.

Research and Sources

Of course, the characters—their traits, language, etc.—have to fit the time and location of the story; therefore, extensive research is done on any topic Hesse chooses. Of her nine books for young adult readers, all but two are historical fiction. She loves to research and prefers her books to be set in the twentieth century because of the wealth of primary sources. The one exception to this choice is *Stowaway* which is set in the late 1700s. But for this book she had access to journals of Captain James Cook and Joseph Banks, a naturalist who was aboard the *Endeavour* during its famous voyage.

When Hesse speaks of primary sources, she may mean archives, journals, books, or back issues of newspapers and periodicals. Or she may be referring to people. A favorite type of research is the interview. Talking with Leonard Marcus, Hesse says she loves to do them—talking with people who have lived during that time is so special. *A Time of Angels* was conceived from pieces she wrote about angels for a friend who was having surgery. The poems, vignettes, and stories were not meant to be published. They were to "surround her friend with angels" during the surgery and recovery time. Hesse had forgotten about these angel pieces until her daughters—who sometimes go through her computer files—found and read them. Kate and Rachel quickly found one piece they especially liked and suggested that it needed to be a book. Hesse sent the story to her editor and the editor agreed with Kate and Rachel. But a six-page story does not constitute a book so the manuscript needed to be expanded. While watching television Hesse saw a documentary on the 1918–1919 influenza epidemic and decided that this would be the vehicle through which to tell her angel story.

Boston was chosen as the setting. In order to get primary sources, Hesse advertised in a national publication for senior citizens. In the advertisement she asked for anyone who could share stories of life in Boston during this specific time period. She received seventy replies with stories, and many made their way into *A Time of Angels*. Not only did she get primary sources for her book, she also made friends. Hesse corresponded with some of the people for several years after the project was complete.

Drafting

This first draft is expanded and revised—a few pages at a time—until the entire manuscript is completed. Hesse says this process goes through a minimum of five drafts. In response to the sharing of her work in draft form Hesse says that she doesn't want others reading the work until she is completely satisfied with it. She does belong to a writer's group and may share an idea or an entire draft with them, but her usual response is not to share until the book is complete. Hesse also has expert readers going over the book looking for errors. The other exception to this rule is Kate and Rachel. In a Scholastic Homepage interview, Hesse says that she began sharing her works in progress to her daughters when they reached an age where they could "articulate things about writing." When they were younger she read the manuscripts to them, but now of course they read the drafts themselves. "They are very helpful in assessing my work's strengths and weaknesses. They are tough reads!"[32]

The Daily Routine

Her writing schedule is an arduous one. When she first began writing in the early 1980s she would get up at 2:00 a.m. to write for four hours before she had to get Kate and Rachel ready for school. Once the girls got older her hours for writing changed somewhat—she'd begin writing at 5:00 a.m., but with her office at home she still found herself writing through the night. She says she'd wake up in the middle of the night, go to her office, turn on the computer, and work until dawn or later. This, of course, caused her to be grumpy the next day, so she decided to move her office out of the house. Her office was moved to the apartment/office in Brattleboro several miles from the Hesse home in Williamsville. Ellen Huntington Bryant in an article about Hesse says the office was "every middle-aged mother's dream—a homey place of one's own away from home."[33] This office had all the amenities of home—a kitchen, living room, and bedroom for any late-night or early-morning writing. There was also a balcony that overlooked the Connecticut River and the mountains of New Hampshire. But since their relocation to Brattleboro she is again working out of her home—the 1880 Queen Anne house.

Hesse says she loves to write and can't wait to get to her desk each morning. She wishes that all people enjoyed their profession as much as she enjoys writing. But she continues to say that writing isn't easy, that she works long hours, and that everything she writes isn't satisfying. When something she writes disappoints her, she throws it out. On the other hand she says that some of her work that she's pleased with receives little attention from others. But no matter what, she gets up each and every morning and plies her trade.

She now begins her day between 4:30 and 5:30 a.m. One of the first things she does is read and respond to email; then Monday through Friday from 7:30 a.m. until 3:30 p.m. she works on her manuscripts, either writing or revising. Working on a first draft often alters the time schedule. On days she's working on the first draft, she may write until 10:00 or 11:00 at night. Once the story begins to unfold she wants to keep going as long as possible. Taking few breaks and eating standing up are typical of the first draft days. If it's a research day at the library, Hesse is standing at the door when it opens at 9:00 a.m. She'll work until her body—especially her eyes—can hold out no longer. (Most of her reading is done from microfilm.) But when she must leave the library, she returns home and continues to work. Saturday is her day off. And Sunday is used for correspondence—responding to fan mail, etc. Hesse drives herself through this brutal schedule week after week because she loves what she does.

It can take her up to two years to complete a book. She spends months researching and gathering information on the subject so that she can feel confident about the topic once the writing begins. Hesse discusses the concept of "back story" in talking about *Witness*, but she uses it with all her books. Back story refers to all of the details about a person, place, or event that need to be known by the author but never make it into the book. She may not use the information in the text, but she needs it in order to get a correct mindset to move the plot along. Speaking specifically about *Witness*, Hesse says she had to create a detailed map of the town as well as knowing all about Mr. Field, even though he was not a speaking character in the book. She also needed to know about Esther's life in New York and her relationship with her mother before the mother's death. For Leanora, her father's occupation was important as well as her relationship with her mother. Finding out all of this information helps Hesse create believable scenarios for the characters.

Hesse generally writes very quickly, and when she's just begun a manuscript, she'll write through day and night until the first draft is complete. This is very sparse—between thirty and sixty pages. This draft is then read, and she begins adding details to the skeleton of the book. In the revision process she works on pages 1, 2, and 3; and when those are to her satisfaction, she then moves on to the next several pages, working a few pages at a time through a series of drafts until the book is complete.

Once a manuscript goes off to the editor, she'll begin another project. Hesse says that she often has two or three books in the works at the same time. One will be with the editor, she'll be writing on a second one; and she will be doing research for a third.

Lots of Genres and Lots of Styles

Not only does Hesse like to write, she likes to write in different genres, different styles, and for different age groups. Most of her books for young adults are historical fiction while her chapter books for younger readers are realistic fiction. Her picture books for children are realistic except for *The Stone Lamp: Eight Stories of Hanukkah through History*, which is historical fiction. It is in a picture book format; yet the stories are geared toward an older audience.

In her brief career—less than fifteen years—as a writer for children and young adults, Hesse has published seventeen books and one short story. *Letters from Rifka, Phoenix Rising, A Time of Angels, The Music of Dolphins, Out of the Dust, A Light in the Story: The Civil War Diary of Amelia Martin, Stowaway, Witness,* and *Aleutian Sparrow* are for the young adult audience. *Wish on a Unicorn* and *Just Juice* are for intermediate readers while *Lavender* and *Sable* are transition chapter books for younger readers. *Poppy's Chair, Lester's Dog,* and *Come on, Rain* are picture books to be shared with beginning readers. Hesse's latest book is also a picture book, but she suggests that *The Stone Lamp: Eight Stories of Hanukkah through History* is for everyone—younger children will love the stories about lighting the candles while older readers will enjoy the history that surrounds this Jewish tradition. The short story "Waiting for Midnight" is an autobiographical piece in the collection *When I Was Your Age,* edited by Amy Ehrlich.

One aspect of Hesse's writing that has constantly amazed readers, reviewers, and critics is her ability to write in so many different styles. The picture books, *Poppy's Chair, Lester's Dog,* and *Come On, Rain,* along with the transition chapter books and intermediate reader chapter books, *Lavender, Sable, Wish on a Unicorn,* and *Just Juice,* are written in narrative prose form. Hesse's only young adult novel to be written in narrative prose is *Phoenix Rising. Letters from Rifka,* Hesse's first book for young adults, is written in letter format. Even though Rifka realizes she cannot mail her letters to Cousin Tovah, she still uses this as a way of chronicling her family's emigration from Russia. In *A Time of Angels* Hannah keeps a journal of her family's life, as does Amelia in *A Light in the Storm: The Civil War Diary of Amelia Martin.* Hesse gives us a different variation on the diary in *Stowaway.* In this story Nicholas Young keeps a ship's log to tell about his experience on the *Endeavour*—the ship that was to map the coasts of New Zealand and Australia. *The Music of Dolphins* is written through Mila's voice. It is prose, but the sixty-two short entries read like a journal.

The book that has brought Hesse and her writing the greatest recognition is *Out of the Dust.* Winner of the 1998 Newbery Award, *Out of the Dust* tells the story of Billie Jo Kelby and her family during the Dust Bowl days of the 1930s in Oklahoma. Hesse says that the only way she could help her readers understand the sparseness of life during that time was to write the story with the fewest words possible. Writing in free verse she accomplished her goal.

Six years after the publication of *Out of the Dust*, Hesse published *Aleutian Sparrow*, the story of the Aleut's relocation during World War II. Again this is a story that is stark and raw and needs few words to explain the situation. In 2001 Hesse tried another format to tell the story of the Ku Klux Klan in Vermont in the 1920s. In deciding how best to show all sides of this conflict, Hesse chose to write a play with each character's voice relaying feeling and opinions in free verse poetry. On her varying styles of writing Hesse says the topics she chooses "just seem to demand a different" writing than straight prose.

It really doesn't matter what genre or style Hesse is using, or for which age group she is writing. She succeeds in all areas. Hesse believes that young readers—her readers—are the most "challenging, demanding, and rewarding audiences."[34] Of her occupation as a writer Hesse says she is fortunate "not only to live my own life but to spend my days recording what it's like to live someone else's—someone from another culture, another economic strata, another belief system, another time."[35] As for her profession, she can't think of anything she'd rather do. And as for her audience she can't think of anyone she'd rather write for.

Notes

1. Karen Hesse, "Newbery Medal Acceptance," *Horn Book Magazine* 74, no. 4 (July/August 1998): 422–427.

2. "Karen Hesse," *Eighth Book of Junior Authors and Illustrators*, ed. Connie C. Rockman. (NY: H.W. Wilson Company, 2000), 217.

3. "Karen Hesse," *Eighth Book*, 217.

4. Alan Hedblad, ed., "Karen Hesse," in *Something about the Author* 113. (Farmington, MI: Gale Group, 2000), 82.

5. Lois T. Stover, "Karen Hesse," *Writers for Young Adults*, ed. Ted Hipple (NY: Charles Schribners and Sons, 2000), 94.

6. Brenda Bowen, "Karen Hesse," *Horn Book Magazine* 74, no. 4. (July/August 1998): 428.

7. Karen Hesse, "Newbery Medal Acceptance," 422.

8. Judy O'Malley, "Talking with . . . Karen Hesse," Book Links 9 no. 1 (September 1999): 56.

9. Karen Hesse, *The Music of Dolphins* (NY: Scholastic Signature, 1996), 33.

10. Judy O'Malley, "Talking with . . . Karen Hesse," 56.

11. Judy O'Malley, "Talking with . . . Karen Hesse," 56.

12. "Karen Hesse: 1998 Newbery Award Winner," Brooks Memorial Library, www.state.vt.us/libraries/b733/ BrooksLibrary.featured_author.htm.

13. Judy O'Malley, "Talking with . . . Karen Hesse," 56.

14. Judy O'Malley, "Talking with . . . Karen Hesse," 57.

15. William McLoughlin, *School Library Journal* 46, no.11 (2000): 156.

16. "Karen Hesse's Interview Transcript," Scholastic Author Studies Homepage, www2.scholastic.com/teachers/authorsandbooks/authorstudies/authorhome.jhtml, February 2, 2004.

17. Ilene Cooper, "Story behind the Story: Hesse's *The Stone Lamp*," *Booklist* (October 2003): 335.

18. Ilene Cooper, "Story behind the Story," 335.

19. *Publisher's Weekly* 244 no. 35 (1997): 72

20. *Kirkus Reviews* (August 1, 2001)

21. *Something about the Author*, "Karen Hesse," 69.

22. *Something about the Author*, "Karen Hesse," 69.

23. *Something about the Author*, "Karen Hesse," 77.

24. "Karen Hesse," *Eighth Book*, 217.

25. "Karen Hesse," *Eighth Book*, 217.

26. "Karen Hesse," *Eighth Book*, 217.

27. Ellen Huntington Bryant, "Honoring the Complexities of Our Lives: An Interview with Karen Hesse," *Voices from the Middle* 4, no. 2 (1997): 39.

28. Cathy Beck, Linda Gwyn, Dick Koblitz, Anne O'Connor, Kathryn Mitchell Pierce, and Susan Wolf, "Talking About Books: Karen Hesse," *Language Arts* 76 (January 1999): 264.

29. Cathy Beck et al., "Talking About Books: Karen Hesse," 264.

30. Judy Hendershot and Jackie Peck, "Newbery Medal Winner, Karen Hesse, Brings Billie Jo's Voice *Out of the Dust*," *The Reading Teacher* 52 (1999): 856.

31. Scholastic Online Reading Club, http://teacher.scholastic.com/ authorsandbooks/events/hesse/Karen_Hesse_transcript.htm, (14 November 2002).

32. "Karen Hesse's Interview Transcript," Scholastic Author Studies Homepage.

33. Bryant, "Honoring the Complexities of Our Lives: An Interview with Karen Hesse," 39.

34. "Karen Hesse," KidsReads.com 2001, www.Kidsreads.com/authors/au-hesse-karen.asp.

35. "Karen Hesse," *Eighth Book*, 217.

Chapter 3

Books: Friends Forever

Some of us grew up listening to stories around the dinner table, on the front porch, or at family gatherings. When we heard these family stories, we were entertained because we knew the characters and could relate to their actions, antics, adventures, accomplishments, and/or shortcomings, and we learned about life. Karen Hesse's books make us feel like we are listening to family stories because we become so engrossed in her characters' lives. Listening to family stories, we also learned about our cultural mores and about caring for one another. In today's fast-paced lifestyle we seem to have lost some of this togetherness. So with the geographical and social breakdown of the family, Hesse's stories give today's readers an opportunity to learn these lessons vicariously. She gently nudges her readers to understand about prejudices and bigotry in all forms. Tolerance of others is a common thread that runs through all of her books. She expands horizons by letting the reader live through her characters and their stories, making choices and living the consequences. Hesse's readers learn that we are truly a world community and need to take care of each other and our environment, and at the same time we are being entertained.

Historical Fiction

Hesse was once told "that writing historical fiction was a bad idea. No market for it."[1] Thank goodness Hesse chose to ignore this advice and do what she loves to do—research. As George Santayana said, "Those who forget history are doomed to repeat it." Reading her historical fiction helps the reader remember—or in many cases learn about—what has happened and be conscious that these mistakes are not made again.

Hesse says historical fiction also teaches that there aren't always set answers. The reader needs to accept that closure doesn't always come, or if it does, it might not be what is expected or even wanted. But reading historical fiction will help the reader grow, and in growth comes understanding and forgiveness.

Books in Free Verse

Out of the Dust

The book most frequently associated with Karen Hesse is her 1998 Newbery Award winner *Out of the Dust*. She already had nine books in print when *Out of the Dust* was written; and all of these books had won awards, received great reviews, and were generally recognized as outstanding; but *Out of the Dust* was different.

Ellen Fader, chair of the Newbery Committee in 1998 says, "Hesse's painstaking first person narration of Billie Jo's withering and, finally taking root, is spare and gritty. She creates a stark and piercing rhythm with free-verse form that naturally and immediately communicates this story of Billie Jo's fierce spirit and growing self-understanding."[2] Young adult readers took to *Out of the Dust* as quickly as did the reviewers. A fourteen-year-old girl wrote a list of what she liked about the book in an online review:

- This book is what writing should be about
- Every word means something
- Every word is important
- Writing it in poem (sic) made it much more real and to the point
- There were no unnecessary sentences between the stanzas
- It was easy to read
- I liked it because it was good and my friends liked it because they

could understand it
- The ending wasn't perfect—it was real
- This story could have actually happened
- I couldn't think of possible endings. I usually have them figured out by the third chapter.

This teenager finishes her list by saying, "Thank you Karen Hesse for writing what is real."[3]

In 2004, six years after *Out of the Dust* won the prestigious New-bery Award, this book is still getting accolades for its contribution to adolescent literature. *Out of the Dust* is listed as one of "The 20th Century's Most Significant English-Language Books for Children and Young Adults" by School Library Journal.[4] Ted Hipple, Professor of Adolescent Literature at the University of Tennessee, Knoxville, is finding that many knowledgeable people who deal with adolescent literature are putting *Out of the Dust* on their lists of the six to eight most influential books for teenagers. Obviously many people are agreeing that this book will make a difference in the reader's life.

A *Booklist* starred review says that *Out of the Dust* "is a powerful tale of a girl with enormous strength, courage, and love."[5] *Publisher's Weekly* says "Hesse's spare prose adroitly traces Billie Jo's journey in and out of darkness."[6] Fourteen-year-old Billie Jo Kelby must use all of this strength, courage, and love to endure the tragedies that life sends her over a year's time. In the fall of 1934, Billie Jo, along with Ma and Daddy, is trying to survive the drought and windstorms that are making the panhandle of Oklahoma a desolate place to live. Though times are hard, the Kelby's have the love of their family and friends to sustain them through these rough, raw, and lean years. In the face of the dying land, Ma is expecting, and Billie Jo is excited to have a younger sibling to love and care for. A freak accident—Ma accidentally pours kerosene into a pot on a hot stove thinking it is water—destroys the family and Billie Jo's hopes for the future. Ma and the baby die; Billie Jo's hands are burned; and blame replaces the love Billie Jo and Daddy once had.

In an interview after *Out of the Dust* won the Newbery, Hesse said if she were to write this book again, she'd put more hope in the earlier part of the book. After the award was announced, Hesse was on her way to do an interview on the *Today* show and decided she needed to reread the book so that she could respond to questions she might be asked. It was at this reading that she realized how sad *Out of the Dust* was. Though the book ends with hope for Billie Jo and Daddy, Hesse says she'd make the beginning less bleak.

Some reviewers questioned the harshness of the story—Ma and the baby's death, Billie Jo's losing the use of her "piano playing" hands, and the blame and conflict that comes between Billie Jo and Daddy. Hesse's response comes in her Newbery acceptance speech. "I never make up any of the bad things that happen to my characters. I love my characters too much to hurt them deliberately, even the prickly ones. It just so happens that in life, there's pain; sorrow lives in the shadow of joy, joy in the shadow of sorrow. The question is, do we let the pain reign triumphant or do we find a way to grow, to transform, and ultimately transcend our pain?"[7]

Readers have asked Hesse if this terrible tragedy of kerosene being mistaken for water could have really happened. It did happen. Hesse based this part of the story on a series of articles that she read in the *Boise City News* from 1934. But she also gives a more recent and personal example. Hesse says Randy is the gardener in the family while she definitely is not. In trying to do her husband a favor, she accidentally watered one of his favorite plants with vinegar. She thought the clear liquid in the bottle was water and didn't realize differently until the smell hit her. The plant died, but Randy forgave Karen just as Billie Jo learns to forgive herself and Pa.

The origins of this book are as unique as the book itself. Hesse says that the idea for the book came from a trip she took with a friend. (Remember her addiction to car trips after her childhood.) In driving across the country en route to Colorado, she and Liza Ketchum from the writing group drove through Kansas and "something extraordinary happened."[8] During the two days it took to cross Kansas, Hesse and Liza witnessed a tornado, the sky changing colors and the air swelling with explosive energy, and visited a town "so small it didn't have a name."[9] The wind never stopped blowing and the land and sky seemed to fuse together. Hesse was entranced with the land and its strange weather.

Out of the Dust didn't get written immediately after this experience. It took her three years, another book, and the query of a member of her writing group to jump start *Out of the Dust*. The other book was what turned out to be *Come on, Rain*—which was not published until 1999. Hesse had shared the manuscript for this picture book about a little girl who desperately wants it to rain with the members of her writing group, and Eileen Christelow—one of the group members—asked the simple question, "Why does this child want it to rain so much?" This question sent Hesse's mind back to that trip through Kansas and back sixty years to the Dust Bowl era when "people desperately wanted rain."[10]

Hesse continues this story by bringing in her editor Brenda Bowen. A few weeks after Eileen's query, Bowen, in a telephone conversation, asked Hesse what her latest project was. She replied that she was "researching agricultural practices on the Great Plains."[11] Hesse remembers that the "silence on the other end of the line was deadly."[12] But Bowen finally broke the silence and her response gave Hesse the impression that "agricultural practices on the Great Plains" was an acceptable topic. Hesse says, "Brenda trusted me. She had faith that if I was excited by dust, there was a good chance she, and ultimately, young readers, would be, too."[13] And Bowen was correct. Hesse's excitement about dust was catching.

Bowen's comments on reading *Out of the Dust* for the first time showed that her faith in Hesse's abilities were on target. While reading, "I was in Oklahoma in 1934. I was tasting the grit in my mouth."[14] Reviewers have referred to Hesse's "astute and careful descriptions" and her ability to "paint a vivid picture" that put her readers in the character's place.

As noted earlier, research is an important part of Hesse's writing. Research for most of her books begins in the children's room of the Brattleboro public library. After reading the books available on the subject, she then uses the footnotes and bibliographies from these to expand her search. The small ripple eventually becomes an ocean of information. For *Out of the Dust*, Hesse found reference to the *Boise City News*, a daily newspaper that was published during the 1930s in Oklahoma. She then contacted the Oklahoma Historical Society to validate the existence of this paper. The paper indeed did exist and could be read on microfilm, which Hesse ordered and upon its arrival proceeded to read. What she found in the stories and articles became the basis of her story. She learned that life continued for the people— rain or shine—and since there was a lot more shine than there was rain, people went about their daily chores. There were dances, talent shows, and movies. Neighbors continued to show neighborly kindness and generosity to each other and to strangers. Weather might be a deterrent, but it couldn't stop them from living.

But why tell this story in free verse? Hesse says that the sparseness of life, the raw emotions, the lack of anything extra had to be portrayed, and this type of writing did exactly these things. "The frugality of life, the hypnotically hard work of farming, the grimness of conditions during the dust bowl, demanded an economy of words."[15]

An interesting observation regarding Hesse and Bowen is their obvious ability to work together and think along the same lines. Hesse used a picture of Lucille Burroughs as the inspiration for Billie Jo Kelby. Hesse kept this picture in a prominent place while she was writing and gives credit to "Lucille Burroughs, who stared out at me from the pages of *Let Us Now Praise Famous Men*, imploring me to tell her story, even if I had to make it up."[16] Bowen chose the same picture of Lucille Burroughs for the cover of the book, not knowing that Hesse was using Lucille's picture as her inspiration.

When asked about the likelihood of a sequel, Hesse doesn't give her readers much hope. She enjoys creating "fiction fresh from the ground up."[17] A sequel doesn't have the allure of a new book because she's already created the characters, and what she likes to do most is create characters. Hesse says she won't say "never," but the chance of her readers finding out about Billie Jo's life in her older years is not a good one.

Witness

Five years after *Out of the Dust*, in 2001, Hesse published her fourteenth book, and *Witness* became her second book to be written in free verse. As noted earlier, the idea for *Witness* came from an article in an airline magazine. After reading it she tore the article out of the magazine and carried it home with her. This bit of information "totally captivated her and took her breath away."[18] Hesse couldn't believe that the Ku Klux Klan came as far north as Vermont or believe that the people of Vermont—always so independent minded—would accept this group. "It blew me away. I had no idea Vermont had hosted the Klan during that period."[19] Rather than beginning at the children's room of the local library for this information, she went directly to her computer for validation. Once this fact was confirmed, she began reading (and watching) everything she could find on the Klan during the 1920s. The first book she read was *Fiery Crosses in the Green Mountains: The Story of the Ku Klux Klan in Vermont* by Maudean Neill. Neill interviewed people from the time period—from Klan members to just ordinary citizens. She read every piece of nonfiction, and then fiction that was available for this particular time period, what Hesse refers to as the Klan's second coming—the first being just after the Civil War. She needed to find out exactly how widespread the Klan was in Vermont and the reactions of the people. Some of the towns were accepting of the KKK; others would have nothing to do with them; and there were many in between. So as she put together her cast of characters—people who might have lived in a small Vermont town in the 1920s—she realized that there would have to be different personalities, different ideas, and different mind sets.

The story that came from this research tells about Leanora and Esther and how their lives are affected—along with the rest of the town—when the KKK tries to enlist members. Leanora is twelve years old, and she and her father are the only blacks in town. Six-year-old Esther is a "Fresh Air" child from New York City. Esther loves Sara Chickering's farm so much that upon returning to New York, she runs "back to Vermont." Her father agrees to this relocation, making them the only Jews in this small town. Some of the town people have chosen, up until the Klan arrives, to ignore or tolerate both these young girls. But with the coming of the Klan, Leanora and Esther begin to feel the full impact of the underlying prejudice of many of their neighbors.

Written in free verse, each character's personality moves the story along. The eleven characters in the play fall in to different categories. Leanora and Esther are the outcasts. Merlin Van Tornhout and Johnny Reeves are the radical racists. Reynard Alexander, the newspaper editor, is liberal. The other characters are less emphatic in their beliefs. They are the ones the Klan wants to sway. Hesse says that these characters are not the "movers and shakers" of the world. In the story she wanted to capture "the simple, homely details of life experienced by ordinary people, going about their days, telling the stories closest to their hearts."[20] The characters who don't have strong beliefs either way are the ones who might be most likely to succumb to subtle pressure from an outside force.

Hesse wanted to tell this story, but couldn't seem to get a handle on exactly how it should be written. In an email from her editor at that time, Jean Feiwel, Hesse was reminded of *Spoon River Anthology* and immediately knew she had the format she needed. Hesse remembered her high school days when she had done *Spoon River Anthology* as reader's theater. But the title became another problem. At first it was titled *Train to Heaven*, (Esther tries to stop a train because she believes her mother was taken to heaven on a train when she died), but Jean Feiwel came through with another idea—a new title—*Witness*. Hesse liked this because she had originally set the story in a courtroom. She confides that the characters were to be the "witnesses" because "when I first started thinking about this book, I imagined it as a trial before the Highest Authority."[21] Feiwel has worked with Hesse on several projects. They worked together on *A Light in the Storm* prior to *Witness*, and Feiwel is the editor for Hesse's two soon-to-be published books.

As far as the free-verse style of writing, Hesse says it seemed natural—the right way to tell the story. Since she began her career as a poet back in her college days, she admits, "maybe it was a reversion back to that stage in my life."[22] The poetry she wrote while in college was also narrative. The verse novel may be a natural progression for her—or a regression to a former time. An early draft of the book included 550 poems—way too many for a young adult book. These were edited down to 300 plus, and the final draft contains 132 poems.

The research done for *Witness* was "paper work." She read every word of seven or eight newspapers that could be found from the area and that era. She devoured each newspaper by reading everything, down to the ads. This prolific reading was how she got a feel for the time period. Music was another vehicle for "getting a feel of the times."[23] For *Witness* an engineer from England put together a CD that included only instrumental music from the early 1920s. Hesse would listen to the music, look at her picture board, and create.

For this particular book Hesse did no interviews. *Fiery Crosses in the Green Mountains* by Maudean Neill contained the information needed. Plus, when Neill was contacted, she assured Hesse that all the information that had been collected was in the book. Neill further stated that she doubted any of the people would be willing to do a second interview. So Hesse immersed herself in the writings and music of the time.

In the Neill book there was one story about a Klan family that had taken in a man and his son. Some people in the community thought the man and son were Jewish (even though they weren't) and this assumption led to conflict over "harboring Jews." This incident inspired the addition of Esther and her father just as many of the newspaper articles inspired other incidents in *Witness*.

Witness was very difficult to write—not only because of the eleven different voices, but also for the reason that Hesse had to write from an anti-Semitic and racist viewpoint. She had to remember that these people lived and loved like everyone, and she needed to respect them as people even if they didn't reciprocate. Still, she says it was "gut wrenching" to write.

When asked about specific happenings in this book—Hesse says that the details are correct. There really was a Fresh Air Program (there still is) that brought children from New York City every summer to "breathe the fresh air" and then returned them to their homes at the end of the summer. Hesse even found an ad in one newspaper asking for volunteers to take these children in. The black population in Vermont would have been very small, but it would have been there, and the other personalities she creates definitely fit into any gathering of people, large or small.

Aleutian Sparrow

Hesse's third book written in free verse is *Aleutian Sparrow*. The idea for the novel came to Hesse from a speaking engagement in Juneau and Ketchikan, Alaska. The people were gracious, making her experience extraordinary. The children with whom she spoke urged her to write a book about Alaska. In order to fulfill their requests, Hesse purchased two boxes of books and had them shipped to Vermont. As she read through the books, she found an anecdote about the Japanese-American evacuation to relocation camps. While delving into this issue, she unearthed the deeply buried Aleut story. Hesse explains, "This story, I feared, might not be told if I didn't give it a try."[24] One of her sources for the book was a gentleman named Ray Hudson. Hesse explains that Hudson "spent many years teaching on the Aleutians. He now lives in Vermont. In my early research for *Aleutian Sparrow* I read a book written by Ray called *Moments Rightly Placed*. When I read the back flap and realized the author was a fellow Vermonter, I tracked him down and asked if he would help me on the project as an expert reader. We met and communicated by mail over the two or so years it took me to complete the book. Ray understood the Aleuts in a way I never could. His assistance made all the difference in the authenticity of *Aleutian Sparrow*."[25]

An aspect of American history of which most people are unaware is the relocation of the Aleuts from their homes during World War II. Much has been written about the Japanese internment camps, but the Aleuts' story hasn't been told. The relocation was done for their safety. Japan attacked the North American continent by bombing Unalaska Island in the Aleutian chain. American military personnel were sent to protect this area, and the government thought this could be done better if they didn't have to worry about also protecting the Aleuts. Moving them to the mainland seemed a perfect solution. But solutions are rarely perfect, and the Aleuts were the ones who suffered.

Hesse says that *Aleutian Sparrow* is a "work of fiction based on true events. The Aleut characters described here are not intended to depict specific individuals, but rather to represent the experience shared by many during the three-year relocation."[26] The story is told through the voice of Vera, a young girl who has been abandoned by both of her parents. Her father, who is white, leaves on his fishing boat and never returns. Whether he is lost at sea or leaves intentionally, Vera never finds out. Her mother, on the other hand, chooses to separate herself from Vera. At first Vera is sent to live with an older couple, Alexie and Fekla, to help them and to attend school, but after the relocation Vera's mother chooses to stay in Ketchican. She tells Vera about the room she's found—a room just large enough for one person and well heated. Two of the many things the Aleuts have not had during their relocation are privacy and sufficient heat in their living quarters. At this time Vera says she's never felt more forsaken, but she realizes that her family is the Aleut community and that she will be well taken care of.

For a people who have for centuries made their living from the water, being relocated where they can see nothing but trees is a difficult transition. Added to this are substandard food and living quarters. Several families must live in one small cabin, and their rations are "chum salmon, tea, and bread, over and over, each day like the day before."[27] The people in nearby Ketchikan do not react kindly to having the Aleuts forced on them, so prejudices become a major issue.

Hesse writes in her author's note that as many as one in four evacuees died from 1942 to 1945 from tuberculosis, whooping cough, measles, mumps, and pneumonia. Many of these diseases were brought on by the substandard living conditions and some by exposure to a new environment. Again the stark and sparse living conditions of the Aleuts fit better with Hesse's free-verse style.

Letters, Diaries, and Journals

Hesse created four of her books using a ship's log, a diary, a journal, and letters. The following four books were written over a span of eight years with other books interspersed. *Letters from Rifka* was written first; *A Time of Angels* followed three years later; *A Light in the Storm: The Civil War Diary of Amelia Martin* came four years later with *Stowaway* following the next year. Discussions of these books will be presented chronologically by the time settings of their stories.

Stowaway

It was a lecture at the local library on the artwork created aboard the *Endeavour* by Sydney Parkinson, who did illustrations of the animals and plants discovered on the voyage, that brought the young stowaway Nicholas Young and Hesse together. Among the sources David Bisno, the lecturer, brought with him was Captain James Cook's journal. The journal was over one thousand pages of pure delight for Hesse. She says Nicholas Young was a mere footnote in the journal. But that is all Hesse needed to create this wonderful story.

The book that *School Library Journal* compared to a "virtual encyclopedia of life in the days when England ruled the seas"[28] and *Publisher's Weekly* calls "a narrative with a wealth of detail"[29] is also a favorite of Hesse's many readers. Nicholas Young's story of being a stowaway on the *Endeavour*, that famous ship captained by James Cook, is one of adventure and caring. The reader first meets Nicholas Young as a stowaway, but his story begins much earlier. After his mother's death Nicholas had gone to live with his grandmother, but she soon also died. When he had returned to his home, it was obvious that his father wanted nothing to do with him. For several years Nicholas had been sent to boarding schools, but after he was expelled from several, his father had decided to apprentice him to a butcher. In 1768, at the age of eleven, Nicholas makes a bold decision—a decision that he will come to question before the end of the three years it takes this ship to return to England. What he envisioned as a way of getting away from his harsh life gets even harsher.

Nicholas pays three seamen to smuggle him aboard the *Endeavour*. His hiding place is in the lifeboats. His only freedom from this confining place is at night when one of his friends is on watch. His food is whatever can be sneaked to him by his "friends." At first being confined in hiding with only leftover food seems like a terrible predicament, but when he is discovered and has to join the crew, his life becomes as unbearable as it was before he boarded the ship. The physical and emotional cruelty that made him leave his home and apprenticeship is nothing compared to the abuse he receives from the crewmembers. Mr. Bootie, one of the midshipmen, takes an immediate dislike to Nicholas and spends much of his time trying to make Nicholas's life miserable with constant verbal and physical abuse. Hesse does an outstanding job of giving the reader deep insight into how people who have no control over their own lives take this frustration out on others.

Dr. Monkhouse, the ship's surgeon; Joseph Banks, a naturalist who is on the voyage to study the flora and fauna to be found in various parts of the globe; and eventually Captain Cook take Nicholas under their wings and give him support to withstand Mr. Bootie's abuse. Their support is not only physical and emotional, but also educational and enlightening. When the ship finally returns to England, thanks to these men and Nicholas's many experiences on the voyage, he is a mature fourteen-year-old who will be able to make better and more rational decisions in the future.

A Light in the Storm: The Civil War Diary of Amelia Martin

When Hesse was asked to write for the "Dear America" series, her contribution turned out to be *A Light in the Storm: The Civil War Diary of Amelia Martin*. The story of a young woman who is seeking to find her place in the world of the 1860s is referred to as "deep, literary, and soulful" by one reviewer. Another says that Hesse "holds us in her spell as she reconstructs the past." Educators have given their approval. Several groups have recognized the value of the book, including the National Council for the Social Studies who named it a Notable Social Studies Trade Book for Young Adults.

Hesse says she likes writing in the diary or journal format, and as stated earlier, she enjoys writing historical fiction. So a young girl's diary during the Civil War was a perfect match for the "Dear America" series and Karen Hesse.

The idea for *A Light in the Storm* came from a 1911 *New York Times*. While doing research for another project, Hesse came across an article about Ida Lewis. Hesse refers to this article as a pre-obituary. Lewis was gravely ill, and the *New York Times* ran an article about the remarkable achievements she had accomplished. Hesse was so enthralled by Lewis's story, that she put away the other project and decided to focus all her energies on lighthouses and their keepers.

The story, loosely based on the life of Ida Lewis, one of the first female lighthouse keepers in America, tells about life on Fenwick Island, Delaware, during the first year of the American Civil War. Fifteen-year-old Amelia Martin is a rarity in the 1860s. She has chosen to continue her education by remaining in school longer than is typical for a young woman of that era. In order to continue her studies, she works as the assistant teacher for the younger children at Bayville School. But the thing that makes her so completely different from the other girls is that she prefers working with her father at the lighthouse rather than sewing and cooking with her mother.

Each morning Amelia rows to the mainland for school. After school she likes to visit Uncle Edward at his store and spend time with her friends as well as help with her grandmother's chores. But the highlight of her day is returning to the island and the lighthouse to take her watch from four until nine each evening. This alone would make a wonderful story, but Hesse brings in the conflict that arose all over America during this period—the conflict that surrounded the issue of slavery and the conflict between Amelia's parents.

Amelia, her father, and Uncle Edward are against slavery. But

Amelia's mother, her grandmother, and many of her friends' parents are pro-slavery. This difference of opinion causes conflict in the Martin home as well as in the community. Uncle Edward's store is vandalized; Reni, a good friend, is forbidden to talk with Amelia, and her parents' relationship is strained.

Her work at the lighthouse, the growing friendship with Daniel Worthington, and her diary are what sustain Amelia during this turbulent time. Like young women of today Amelia is trying desperately to assert her independence. Yet she is still in her formative years and needs guidance. The two people she most needs are not there for her. Her mother's illness and her father's reluctance to discuss personal matters with Amelia make it hard for her. Whether Hesse is writing from personal experience relating to her own early adolescent years or not, she handles Amelia's dilemma with her usual grace. For the young women of today who are faced with similar circumstances, Hesse shows that there is hope through their own determination.

A Time of Angels

As a young girl living on West Garrison Avenue, Hesse remembers seeing angels coming down out of the sky. She tells about this miraculous event in her short story "Waiting for Midnight." In the Jewish tradition there is a holiday called Shavuos. Hesse says as a ten-year-old she read a story about K'Tonton, a Jewish Tom Thumb. In this story she discovers that if you make a wish at midnight on Shavuos, it will be granted because the sky will open up and your wish will reach Heaven. During this period Karen's parents were having problems; her mother was ill; and the children next door were being abused by their mother. The young Hesse was trying to contain all of this grief and sorrow within herself. Not feeling comfortable telling her problems—or those of the neighbor children—to an adult, Karen decided to stay awake on Shavuos and make her wish for the people she knew and loved who needed help.

She did manage to stay awake that night in May and watched as "the filmy black of the night split open." Karen saw the "most exquisite colors." There was a "shimmering brightness" and "ladders unfurled. And down those ladders, beings descended. Brilliant beings of light. They were angels. I was seeing angels."[30] In the excitement of what she was seeing, Karen failed to make a wish. She wanted to cry, but no tears would come. Instead, she finally slept. The next morning her parents' problems were still there: her mother was still sick, but the light that woke her up was that of flashing lights on police cars. When Karen looked out her bedroom window, she saw the children being taken out of their house by the police—to safety. Perhaps one of her wishes had ascended to Heaven?

As has been mentioned earlier, many years later a friend was having surgery. When Hesse asked what she could do to help, the response from her friend was to surround her with angels. At this request Hesse wrote the many poems, essays, vignettes, and stories about angels that her daughters found in her computer and suggested that one specific story would make a great book. In 1995 Hesse's third book for adolescents, *A Time of Angels*, was published.

Hannah Gold is a spunky fourteen-year-old who must take on the responsibility of her two younger sisters, Libbie and Eve. Their parents have returned to Russia—their mother to take care of her ailing mother and their father to help fight the Bolsheviks during World War I. The girls are living with their great-aunt Tante Rose and her companion, Vashti. Tante Rose lovingly accepts her nieces into her home, but Hannah realizes that Vashti would prefer they not be there. So when Tante Rose dies from the influenza, Hannah has to make a very difficult decision—whether or not to leave her sisters to the care of Vashti. Ill herself, Hannah leaves Boston in order to stay with relatives in upstate New York but ends up in Vermont under the care of a German immigrant named Klaus Gerhard. The guiding force that sees her through this time is "the girl with the violet eyes"—her guardian angel.

Letters from Rifka

In 1992 *Letters from Rifka*, Hesse's second book, but her first for an adolescent audience, was published. The idea for this book came from her great-aunt Lucy. In the Author's Note at the beginning of *Letters from Rifka*, Hesse says her intent was to write a story about her family's emigration from Russia to America. As a child she'd heard the family stories about her grandmother's "wearing white kid gloves as she rode through Poland in the back of an oxcart"[31] and that her grandfather had sold his ticket on the *Titanic* to someone who offered him more money than the face value of the ticket.

Not remembering any other specifics of the family's journey to America, Hesse called her mother and aunts for their assistance. She says they "contributed a wealth of stories about their own childhood,"[32] but they didn't have any new information about the family's emigration. Finally, her mother suggested that she call her great-aunt Lucy, and this communication was the beginning of a wonderful story. Lucy responded to Hesse's written request for information—a list of questions—via a tape. When the tape arrived, Hesse quickly put it in the tape player, and for five minutes she listened as great-aunt Lucy spoke at "breakneck speed." Hesse says listening to Aunt Lucy tell her story was like riding on a roller coaster while holding on for dear life. The tale Hesse heard in that very short tape intrigued her, and she immediately knew that this story was not all great-aunt Lucy had to tell. Hesse decided a visit was in order so that she could interview this lady and hear all of her wonderful narrative. Hesse says that when she called to ask about coming to visit to get more information, great-aunt Lucy's response was "I knew I'd be hearing from you again!" Hesse describes her great-aunt as a "tiny woman with an unruly bun of snow-white hair on top of her head."[33] And even though Hesse doesn't come right out and say it, the reader just knows that great-aunt Lucy is a combination of those feisty, witty, wise, and eccentric aunts that we all love. An afternoon's visit with this vivacious lady gave Hesse the impetus for *Letters from Rifka*. Hesse tells us, "I changed names and adjusted certain details, but this story is above all else, Aunt Lucy's story."[34]

Letters from Rifka chronicles the journey of a young Jewish girl and her family who must flee Russia to keep the young adult sons from being conscripted into the Russian army. Rifka at twelve is the youngest child and only daughter in the Nebrot family. Her job in the escape plan is to occupy the Russian soldiers' attention while her parents and brothers hide on the train for an early morning escape. Rifka's blond hair means that she can pass as a Russian peasant girl on her way to become a servant for a wealthy household in another town. Rifka succeeds in keeping the attention away from the train where her family is hiding. After finally reaching the Polish border, Rifka believes she and her family are free. But this is not the case. Rifka contracts ringworm from a girl on the Polish train and is refused passage to America. First, she is detained in Belgium while her ringworm is treated and cured, and then she is detained on Ellis Island because she is bald. The HIAS lady bluntly informs Rifka, "Your lack of hair makes you an undesirable immigrant. They think without hair you will never find a husband to take care of you and so they will have to take care of you instead."[35]

Rifka tells her story through writing letters to her cousin Tovah, whom she has left behind in Russia. The letters are written in the margins and on the end pages of a collection of Pushkin's works—a parting gift from Tovah.

In a little over a year from September 1919 until October 1920, Rifka matures from a child who thinks she needs to be taken care of into a person who takes control of her own life. As in the real world, this transformation doesn't happen quickly, and it isn't easy. How devastating and traumatic it must have been to be left in a strange land with strangers. Rifka's reaction is typical—she begs and pleads. And when this doesn't work, she withdraws into her own world. But with the love and acceptance shown to her by Sister Katrina and Marie and Gaston in Antwerp, Pieter on the ship, and Nurse Bowen on Ellis Island, Rifka begins to realize how much alike people are no matter what their backgrounds. The love and acceptance that she received from these people she bestows on Ilya. The cycle of taking care of one another is once again complete.

Realistic Fiction

Phoenix Rising

One of the two young adult books Hesse has written in the genre of realistic fiction is *Phoenix Rising*. This is the story of nuclear disaster about which Hesse's agent had concerns when told of the idea. *Publisher's Weekly* gave *Phoenix Rising* a starred review and called it a "searching and memorable tale." The impetus for this story came from a television documentary. While watching "The Children of Chernobyl" Hesse began to realize the scope of the devastation done when in 1986 the Chernobyl nuclear power plant had its meltdown. Thirty people were killed from the explosions, but the effect of the radiation covered an area hundreds of miles away from the power plant. The documentary showed how this disaster affected the communities, the land, the people, and especially the children.

Hesse says she caught the program about midway through, but was so compelled by the images that she couldn't go to sleep. Finally, in the middle of the night, she got up and found the TV portion in the newspaper to see if this documentary would be shown again. To her great relief it was to be rebroadcast the next day. This gave her the opportunity to tape the program. Hesse says she must have watched the tape at least fifteen to twenty times. She was obsessed with the idea of nuclear disaster and its effects on the people and the environment.

"I was totally obsessed. I couldn't let it go. Well, you know what writers do when they're obsessed with something—they write about it."[36] (Her obsession might have something to do with the fact that the Vermont Yankee nuclear power plant is located in Vernon, Vermont.) As always, Hesse did her research on the topic and chose to set the story in Vermont. She continues telling about the beginnings of *Phoenix Rising* by saying that she wrote a "very intense piece" and sent it to her agent. Because the agent usually responded quite quickly to any manuscript Hesse sent her, when no word came about the book for several days, Hesse had the feeling that something must be wrong. When the call finally came, the agent did not give a positive response. She even went so far as to suggest that Hesse put her energies in another project.

The first draft of *Phoenix Rising*—or the book that would eventually become *Phoenix Rising*—had its setting in the center of the nuclear disaster, which may have been the cause of her agent's concern about the book. (When Hesse was being interviewed about the book three years after its publication, she agreed that the original story was probably "too intense and upsetting for a young adult novel.")[37] Hesse tried to move on to other projects, but this particular story kept resurfacing in her mind. Finally, she discussed the problem with Randy, and his suggestion was to, "Do it. It doesn't matter if you publish it or not. Get it out of your system."[38]

The first draft had included a "small" scene on a sheep farm, so Hesse had spent a day visiting a sheep farm doing research. The sheep farmer, David Major, had been very kind—letting her join every tour that day and responding to her "thousand" questions. When she decided the setting needed to move from the center of the nuclear disaster, the nuclear power plant, Hesse remembered her visit to the sheep farm and decided this setting would be perfect for the story. This decision to move the setting led to Hesse's going to work on the farm so that she could get an idea of what a working sheep farm is really like. (She really does get into her research!) And the locale of the sheep farm did make the perfect setting for the book. Not only was she able to write about the effects of nuclear disaster on people, but she was also able to include the effects on the land and the animals—the environment. It is the sheep farm owned by David Major and his wife Cindy that we read about in *Phoenix Rising*.

Brenda Bowen agrees that *Phoenix Rising* was a difficult book to edit. She had expected a much more "sensationalized" story, but found that Hesse had done a superb job of creating Nyle's story. Bowen further says that the book that was originally titled *Forever Ezra* "marked a maturity in her writing that we are all now privileged to witness with each new book."[39] Bowen continues that after Hesse pulled off the story about nuclear disaster, she no longer questioned anything this author might desire to write. Speech development or soil erosion in Oklahoma, Bowen knew it would all turn out fine.

There's no such thing as a typical thirteen-year-old. But even if there were, Nyle Sumner would not fit the description. She's been forced to deal with the death of her mother and grandfather and being abandoned by her father. The life she has lived with Gran the past seven years is now turned upside down by an accident at the nuclear power plant in nearby Cookshire. Fear of radiation poisoning from the air or contamination of food, water, and the land put great strains on daily life. Nyle and Gran live on a sheep farm; therefore, they have the animals to worry about as well as concern about their own health. Eight days after the disaster, the radiation level is such that "Mr. Perry, our principal, said as long as the wind kept blowing radiation away from us, we only needed our masks outside."[40] Nyle's taking off the mask is a sign that life will soon get back to normal. But then Gran invites two of the evacuees into their home because Ezra Trent and his mother "have no place to go." Gran explains, "No home. No money. They left everything behind in Cookshire. Everything, Nyle. There's a lot of folks scared of them. Afraid of the radiation they might be carrying."[41] It's not the reaction of the community to the visitors that bothers Nyle the most. It's the fact that Gran has invited Ezra and his mother to stay in the back bedroom, where six years ago her mother died of cancer and two years ago her beloved grandfather also died. What bothers Nyle the most is that she will have to revisit the pain that comes with the back bedroom—the dying room—again.

Not content to deal only with nuclear disaster and death, Hesse also includes prejudice in this story. Muncie, Nyle's friend, is small of stature. Some of the other students make fun of Muncie calling her "Munchkin" and "Dwaft." Nyle continually finds herself having to defend Muncie and at the same time soothe Muncie's insecurities.

The prejudice shown to Ezra and his mother comes from the radiation poisoning and the community's fear of contracting the disease themselves. But some people would have taken in the Trents except for the fact that Mr. Trent—who died from exposure to radiation—was in charge of the nuclear plant.

Nyle realizes that fear is what causes these prejudices in others, but she can't accept that her fear of the dying room is also a form of prejudice. Nyle, like Rifka, matures through the process of watching Ezra's fight for survival, Muncie's realization that she doesn't have to let her disability control her life, and her own acceptance of life and death.

The Music of Dolphins

The only survivor of a plane crash when she is four years old, Mila is stranded on an uninhabited island off the coast of Florida. She is adopted by a dolphin community and learns to live within their social order—even being able to communicate with them. As a teenager she is "rescued" and sent to a research institute in Boston. For Dr. Beck, whose research interests lie in language acquisition and development, Mila is the perfect subject since she is prelingual. Dr. Beck, Sandy, Justin, and Shay replace the dolphin community as Mila's family. Mila progresses in her language and social skills at first, but then begins to regress. Her choice becomes whether to stay with her human family or return to her life with the dolphins.

Hesse says that she did more research for this book than any other she's written. She also wrote and rewrote the ending for this story three times. Mila chooses to return to the dolphins. Hesse's editor was not pleased with this decision and asked her to "consider bringing Mila back to human society." Hesse complied and rewrote, weaving in the needed material to fit this new ending. But when she reread the revised work, Hesse wasn't satisfied. She says, "It didn't feel honest. It didn't have the integrity that it needed to have."[42]

In order to show Mila's language progression, Hesse chose to use font size and syntax. As Mila becomes more fluent in her language the font size becomes smaller and the syntax of her sentences becomes more fluent.

As mentioned earlier the impetus for the story came from NPR. The program discussed Genie, a teenager from California, who had no language because of her environment. Once she was removed from her abusive home and placed in a hospital, speech therapists began to work with her. She was the perfect subject for studying language acquisition. Genie's exploitation by "society" after her abusive background bothered Hesse. As she had with other topics, Hesse became intrigued with feral children, and out of this grew *The Music of Dolphins*.

Notes

1. Karen Hesse, "Newbery Medal Acceptance," *Horn Book Magazine* 74, no. 4 (July/August 1998): 422.

2. ALA News release (January 1998), http://www.ala.org/news /majorawards.html, February 10, 2003.

3. Literature Learning Ladders Classroom Connections website.

4. Karen Breem, Ellen Fader, Kathleen Odear, and Zena Sutherland, "One Hundred Books That Shaped the Century," *School Library Journal* 46, no. 1 (January 2000): 50–58.

5. Susan Dove Lempke, "Review of *Out of the Dust*," *Booklist* 94 (1997): 330.

6. *Publisher's Weekly* 244 no. 35, (1997): 72.

7. Karen Hesse, "Newbery Medal Acceptance."

8. Karen Hesse, "Newbery Medal Acceptance."

9. Karen Hesse, "Newbery Medal Acceptance."

10. Karen Hesse, "Newbery Medal Acceptance."

11. Karen Hesse, "Newbery Medal Acceptance."

12. Karen Hesse, "Newbery Medal Acceptance."

13. Karen Hesse, "Newbery Medal Acceptance."

14. Brenda Bowen, "Karen Hesse," *Horn Book Magazine* 74, no. 4. (July/August 1998): 431–432.

15. Karen Hesse, "Newbery Medal Acceptance."

16. Karen Hesse, "Newbery Medal Acceptance."

17. "Karen Hesse's Interview Transcript," Scholastic Author Studies Homepage, www.scholastic.com/teachers/authorsandbooks/authorstudies/authorhome.jhtml, February 2, 2004.

18. "Karen Hesse," *Eighth Book of Junior Authors and Illustrators*, ed. Connie C. Rockman. (NY: H.W. Wilson Company, 2000), 217.

19. "Interview with Leonard Marcus" Listening Library.

20. Scholastic Online Reading Club, http://teacher.scholastic.com/authorsandbooks/events/hesse/Karen_Hesse_transcript.htm, November 14, 2002

21. Scholastic Online Reading Club.

22. "Interview with Leonard Marcus."

23. "Interview with Leonard Marcus."

24. Karen Hesse, *Aleutian Sparrow* (NY: Simon and Schuster, 2003), 155.

25. Personal email correspondence with Karen Hesse.

26. Karen Hesse, *Aleutian Sparrow*, 155.

27. Karen Hesse, *Aleutian Sparrow*, 34.

28. William McLoughlin, *School Library Journal* 46, no. 11 (2000): 156.

29. *Publisher's Weekly* 247, no. 43 (2000): 75.

30. Karen Hesse, "Waiting for Midnight," *When I Was Your Age: Original Stories about Growing Up* 2nd ed. Amy Ehrlich, (Cambridge, MA: Candlewick Press, 1996).

31. Karen Hesse, *Letters from Rifka* (NY: Puffin Books/Penguin Putnam, 1992), ix.

32. Karen Hesse, *Letters from Rifka*, ix.

33. Karen Hesse, *Letters from Rifka*, x.

34. Karen Hesse, *Letters from Rifka*, x.

35. Karen Hesse, *Letters from Rifka*, 95.

36. Ellen Huntington Bryant, "Honoring the Complexities of Our Lives: An Interview with Karen Hesse," *Voices from the Middle* 4, no. 2 (1997): 40.

37. Ellen Huntington Bryant, *Voices from the Middle*, 40.

38. Ellen Huntington Bryant, *Voices from the Middle*, 40.

39. Brenda Bowen, "Karen Hesse," 431.

40. Karen Hesse, *Phoenix Rising* (NY: Puffin Books/Penguin Putnam, 1994), 11.

41. Karen Hesse, *Phoenix Rising*, 17.

42. Cathy Beck, Linda Gwyn, Dick Koblitz, Anne O'Connor, Kathryn Mitchell Pierce, and Susan Wolf, "Talking About Books: Karen Hesse," *Language Arts* 76 (January 1999): 267.

Chapter 4

Themes

Hesse says if there is one dominate theme that runs through all of her books, it is tolerance. She believes the more tolerant we are with each other, the better place the world becomes. If we are to practice Tikkum Olam, then tolerance has to come to and from a wide variety of people and places. Hesse's books give the reader a glimpse of this tolerance.

Family

The act of becoming part of a family or community is one that we take for granted, as do all of Hesse's characters, until that support system is removed. In her stories, as in real life, families do not always stay intact. One of the strengths of Hesse's books is the ability of her characters to survive—even at times thrive—when the family support is removed. Protagonists in her stories face issues that come with being a part of any family group, trying to keep a family together, accepting new family members, or finding and fitting into the larger community family. In order for these goals to be accomplished, all parties must be tolerant of each other.

In her books Hesse explores all types of families—nuclear, extended, fictive, and community. Her protagonists, like Hesse, begin life with two parents, but again like Hesse, this situation changes for some of these characters by the time we meet them. Some families change drastically while others change a little. Nicholas and Vera are left alone and must create a new family for themselves. Billie Jo, Hannah, Amelia, Nyle, Leonora, and Esther must adapt to a new family structure. Rifka and Mila are the only ones to have the same family at the end of their stories as they did in the beginning.

Billie Jo, Amelia, and Rifka have two parents, yet each one has a different experience with her family. Hannah's parents are not present, but this absence is not by their own choice. Leonora and Esther are being reared by their fathers in one-parent families. Nicholas and Nyle have to deal with the death of their mothers. Nyle, Nicholas, and Vera have fathers who abandon them either physically or emotionally. Vera is also abandoned by her mother. Hannah and Nyle have extended family to take care of them, but Vera and Nicholas must rely on the community for their support. Mila has the most unique family—dolphins—and a fictive family—Dr. Beck and Sandy—after she is rescued.

Billie Jo, Rifka, Hannah, and Amelia have their nuclear family intact, but there are variations to this family makeup throughout their stories. Billie Jo has Ma and Daddy until Ma dies from the accident. Rifka also has both parents but must be separated from them when she is refused passage to America because of the ringworm. Both of Hannah's parents are alive, but circumstances of World War I keep them away from their daughters. Amelia's nuclear family is dissolved when her parents decide to divorce.

Hannah and Nyle become part of an extended family—Hannah by Tante Rose and Nyle by Gran. Mila is cared for by a fictive family—someone who becomes her legal guardian but has no family ties—Dr. Beck and Sandy. Nicholas and Vera have their community as family. Vera has always felt a strong connection to her Aleut roots, and Nicholas learns to appreciate the family that is created by the members of the ship's crew.

As Hesse writes about families in her novels, she might—or might not—be writing from her own experiences. Bryant writing in *Voices in the Middle* says that "many of Karen's stories were inspired by her childhood."[1] As a young child Karen lived with her father, mother, and brother in a nuclear family situation. After her parents' divorce and subsequent remarriages, her family structure changed to include stepparents and siblings. Hesse also speaks fondly of her extended family of grandparents and aunts as well as her community family on West Garrison Avenue. When reading any of Hesse's books, the reader can count on getting to know and understand unique families and different family structures as well as being entertained with a great story.

The Real Heroes

Our ideas about heroines often stem from folk literature: the beautiful fair maiden who is rescued by the handsome prince. Hesse's heroines are not "fair of face," and they don't wait around for a knight in shining armor. Each young woman sees herself realistically. Billie Jo describes herself as a "long-legged girl with a wide mouth and cheekbones like bicycle handles."[2] Amelia talks about chapped hands that aren't very ladylike, and when Daniel asks for a "likeness" of her, she writes about herself in her diary, "There are few more homely on the face of the earth."[3] Hannah would like a smaller nose, while Nyle is concerned about her wispy flyaway hair. For Leanora, it is the color of her skin that makes her unlovely in some peoples' eyes. The second-hand clothes from the discard barrel that Vera and the other Aleuts have to wear after the relocation causes her to feel unlovely. Not until she is acclimated to her "human surroundings" is Mila aware of her physical features. After realizing that she is the person on the television does she talk about "the wild girl with the curtain of salt-crusted hair and the frightened eyes."[4] Rifka is the only protagonist who is described as beautiful. Her long blond curls are her crowning glory, so it is a shock when she loses her hair because of ringworm. What makes these young women heroines is not their looks, but the determination to help themselves, their families, and their communities through whatever hardships that arise.

Hesse also seems to see herself realistically. In *Something about the Author* she describes herself during childhood as having "long skinny legs, buckteeth, tons of freckles, enormous green eyes, and a mop of brown hair."[5] Yet like the characters in her books, Hesse became a strong, self-confident adult who has accomplished much. Sometimes the accomplishments may be more introspective, as with Billie Jo, Nyle, and Hannah. Billie Jo's courageousness appears in her ability finally to accept that Ma's death was an accident and to forgive her father and herself for their actions. She also shows great courage in dealing with her crippled hands. She could have accepted that her music was gone, but with the help of family—Daddy—and the community—Arley and Vera, Mad Dog, Miss Freeland, and Doc Rice—Billie Jo declares that she is again able to "stretch my fingers over the keys"[6] and play her music. Nyle's heroism comes when she accepts the dying room and Ezra's undeniable fate. A real hero, Nyle sits with him until his death. For Hannah an act of heroism is to accept that Vashti can better help Libbie and Eve—knowing when to "let go" is heroism.

Amelia, like her real-life counterpart, Ida Lewis, became one of the first female lighthouse keepers in America. This feat is quite an accomplishment for a woman in the 1800s. Accepting the breakup of her family—divorce in the 1800s was not as common and as accepted as today—also shows her strength of character. Rifka, too, learns to be self-sufficient. It doesn't happen overnight. The readers see the beginnings of this accomplishment when Rifka ventures out in Antwerp. The voyage to America gives her more experience of being on her own; so when she finally is detained on Ellis Island, Rifka is ready to exert her independence. Her declaration to Mr. Fargate regarding her marriage ability, "If I wish to marry, Mr. Fargate. . . . If I wish to marry, I will do so with hair or without hair,"[7] shows how much she has matured from the young girl who is so vain about her blond curls. A true hero, she knows she can take care of herself.

Vera must use all the courage she can muster in order to live through the forced relocation and internment of her people. Not only are they taken out of their element and made to live in a physical environment that is not conducive to their lifestyle, but they also must watch their families and friends become sick and die, as well as endure the prejudices of the people of Ketchican. Their courage is tested to the greatest degree when they return to Unalaska and find the devastation that has been done to their homes and the island. Yet the reader leaves this story knowing that Vera will succeed, and because of her the Aleut culture will survive for many more years. Mila's entire existence is an heroic endeavor, but the courage she shows in adapting to "human society" is tremendous. All of Hesse's protagonists have to make choices about their lives, but Mila's seems the most drastic.

Hesse's one male protagonist is also heroic. When Nicholas is finally able to hold his own with the other seamen, Captain Cook acknowledges his worthiness and officially accepts him as a member of the crew. But Nick's true heroism is evident at the end of the voyage when he chooses to face his nemeses. "Turning for one last look at *Endeavour*, I saw John Ramsay and John Charlton watching me from aloft in the rigging. For one moment I considered running back up the plank to join them. But I stood tall and waved farewell instead. I have things to settle first with Father and the Butcher."[8]

True heroism often comes—as with Hannah—by accepting others and the help they can give. In acceptance there must be tolerance of others' ideas and lifestyles.

Prejudices

It has been said that we are all prejudiced in some way, and this is surely true. Even Karen Hesse admits to being prejudiced. When asked if she had ever struggled with feelings of racism or prejudice, she replied in the affirmative. But she says that with education and experience she has overcome a certain degree of personal ignorance. And we all know that prejudices come from ignorance of or about a person, place, or thing. In educating her readers about different people or experiences, she is addressing prejudices without making her books didactic. She is subtly introducing her readers to the concept of tolerance. Her stories look at prejudice from many perspectives. Leanora and Esther in *Witness*, Rifka in *Letters from Rifka*, and Vera in *Aleutian Sparrow* are the most obvious. These girls collide with a dominant culture that is prejudiced against people who are different due to skin color, religion, or ethnic background.

In her stories Hesse is showing her readers that racial prejudices are not limited to one area of the country or to one country, but are worldwide. Being black in a small town in Vermont in the 1920s was just as daunting as living in the South. For Esther and her father the cause is being Jewish. In the 1920s the Jewish population tended to be in the cities; the discrimination against Jews in small towns was as prevalent as that against blacks. Rifka's story would not have been the same had it not been for the Russian persecution of Jews. This discrimination, of course, is religious. A form of reverse discrimination occurs in *Letters from Rifka* when Saul refuses to accept young Ilya, who is a Russian peasant child, as does Rifka at first. Because the Russians had persecuted him, Saul chooses to show prejudice against Ilya.

During World War II the U.S. government showed its prejudice against several ethnic groups. *Aleutian Sparrow* tells the relocation story of the Aleuts. This move was supposedly done for their protection, but in the forced migration the group was stripped of their dignity. Instead of understanding the culture, the government chose to treat the Aleuts as a people who were less intelligent and to force the "American lifestyle" on them, rather than helping to create a more ethnically compatible living place. The Aleuts were removed from their coastal homes on the Bering Sea and the North Pacific to the land-locked internment camp. This removal not only took away their way of making a living, but also caused illnesses due to the change in climate. Prejudice is also a class issue. The people of Ketchican, many of whom were also from various ethnic backgrounds, saw the Aleuts as being lesser people because of their lifestyle and because they had to dress in discarded second-hand clothes. Furthermore, the people of Ketchican feared the Aleuts because of the competition for jobs.

In *A Light in the Storm* Amelia sees the discrimination that occurs when a community becomes divided over an issue. In Delaware in the mid-1800s the issue was, of course, slavery and the differing views on the Civil War. But in her immediate family it is her mother's perception of social standing in the community—Mr. Martin's demotion from a ship's captain to an assistant lighthouse keeper—that is the issue.

The discrimination in *Phoenix Rising* is not ethnic, racial, or religious. Ezra Trent and his mother are not only victims of the nuclear disaster, which makes people fear contracting radiation poisoning from them; but since Mr. Trent was the head of the nuclear plant, Ezra and his mother are also seen as part of the problem. People are often discriminated against because of their occupation and sometimes because of perceived social standing. In addition, Muncie is discriminated against because of her physical disability.

In *A Time of Angels* the neighbors are prejudiced against Ovadiah because of his refusal to join the army like all the other men in the neighborhood. And Hannah sees prejudice because she is a girl; a girl selling newspapers on the street is not accepted by many. Customers "went out of their way to avoid me. They muttered about girls doing a boy's work,"[9] she sadly laments. The discrimination could be more than simply avoidance by customers. "A girl selling newspapers in Boston could find herself in trouble; newsgirls got beat up, robbed."[10] And Klaus was discriminated against—even though he had been a viable part of the community previously—because of his German heritage after the United States began fighting the Germans.

Fear of the Unknown

We fear what we do not know, and each of Hesse's protagonists has to deal with moving into an area either physically, mentally, or emotionally unknown. Mila, Vera, Rifka, Nicholas, and Hannah have to deal with a new physical environment. Nyle and Billie Jo have to contend with a change in their surroundings. Amelia and Leanora must handle an emotional climate that changes their environment. Sometimes the unknowns can be controlled, and at other times they cannot.

Mila in *The Music of Dolphins* has to suffer the most drastic changes. Having lived all her remembered life as a member of a dolphin family, she is "rescued" and moved to a human environment. Not only are her physical surroundings changed, but she is also forced to deal with a species for which she has no schema. It is difficult for the reader to grasp exactly how drastic this change would have been for Mila, but Hesse does an outstanding job of making the reader empathetic to Mila and her situation.

Vera and her community are relocated from one part of Alaska to another. This transition doesn't seem drastic until the reader understands that the Aleuts were moved from a coastal environment where their ancestors have lived for centuries to an area that is not conducive to their lifestyle. Their freedoms were taken away, and they were treated even more harshly than the German prisoners. An unknown land and unknown lifestyle with no control or choices creates fear, yet Vera's fear of the unknown doesn't end. The internment camp is a new geographical location with new rules, but Vera has her friends and extended family for support. When they return to their home on the Aleutian Islands, their lifestyle must change again because of the damage to the area from the American troops who have been stationed there. Vera's fear now is what will happen to her people.

> Our fishing grounds and beaches slick with oil,
> Our berry patches crushed under the weight of Quonset
> > Huts, our churches looted.
> We cannot eat the war-poisoned clams and mussels; soldiers
> > Murdered our foxes and our sea lions.
> Our very culture stolen or destroyed, not by the enemy, but
> By our own countrymen.[11]

Alone in Belgium, Rifka has a difficult time adapting. Of course, her concerns not only include being away from her family, but she must also deal with a new language, new location, new customs, and the fact that she is bald and that her beloved blond curls may never grow back. When she is finally allowed to immigrate, the officials at Ellis Island use another unknown to make her life even more stressful. Rifka isn't allowed into America—not because of the ringworm, which is now cured—but because the officials are not convinced that a bald-headed woman can "get a husband."

Nicholas has no idea what he is getting into when he pays John Ramsay to sneak him aboard the *Endeavour*. Nicholas has willingly chosen his unknown, but that choice doesn't make his life any easier than that of the other protagonists who are forced into their unknowns.

Hannah's unknown, like Rifka's, is both geographical and cultural.

Hannah has spent the majority of her life in Boston, so the mountains of Vermont are new territory. But it is the cultural differences that seem to be her biggest stumbling blocks. Coming from a close-knit Jewish community in Boston, Hannah finds it difficult to understand the friendship and caring between seemingly diverse people in this new location. Having lived all of her life in a Jewish household, Hannah is confused as to what foods are appropriate for her to eat. This dilemma causes fear for her and concern for Klaus since he doesn't understand why she isn't eating. Hannah must also deal with the unknown of her sisters—are they alive, or did they die from the influenza?

An unknown for both Billie Jo and Nyle is the weather. Unlike the other protagonists, they don't leave their homes, but their homes seem to abandon them. The dust storms turn the Oklahoma landscape into an unknown land. Billie Jo's father doesn't want to change crops; he knows what wheat will do, and any other crops are an unknown.

Like the dust storms in Oklahoma, it is the wind that brings the unknown to Nyle and Gran's Vermont farm. The nuclear meltdown at Cookshire hasn't affected them badly—yet. But a change in the wind could bring the deadly radiation to the farm, killing not only their livestock but also contaminating the ground for generations to come.

For Amelia there are several unknowns. One is her job at the lighthouse, another is the war between the states, but the most important for her is her parents' relationship. As her parents drift further and further apart, neither will confide in Amelia. Knowing that something is amiss, yet not knowing what the problem is makes Amelia's life difficult.

Leanora's life may be the one with the least unknowns. She is black and knows she is hated by some in the community simply because of her race. She knows that Merlin Van Tornhout wasn't the person who tried to kill Esther's father. But what she doesn't know is her own feelings about life and how to respond.

In spite of the difficulty of learning to adapt to new situations, all of Hesse's protagonists overcome fear and mature because of the choices they are forced to make. Mila has to decide whether to stay in the human community or return to live with her beloved dolphins. She no longer fears her new environment or the people in it, but she chooses to return to the life she knows best. "As I stand, looking west, all the world is water and I, with my two strong legs, with my strong heart and my deep lungs, I belong to it."[12]

Vera, like Mila, chooses to return to her former home. She knows it will be hard, and when she and the others arrive in Unalaska, they are confronted with the destruction that has been done to their homes and the environment. Yet she has a positive attitude when she says, "And as Aleuts have always done, we find the will to begin again."[13]

Rifka, in one of the books where everyone does live happily ever after, is reunited with her family. The spoiled younger sister the family left when they set sail for America is now a confident young woman who no longer sees herself as an extension of her family. It is obvious to the reader that Rifka will be leading her brother and her parents as they assimilate into American life. The more unknown the situations to which she is exposed, the stronger she becomes. This may be "Aunt Lucy's story," but there is a definite parallel to Hesse's life. Like Rifka, Hesse seems to take hurdles as a challenge to make herself stronger. When asked about her shyness and being able to fit into a high school setting where teenage girls tend not to be accepting of those not like themselves, Hesse responded that in high school she learned to "compensate."

Nicholas and Rifka have a lot in common. They both begin their stories with an unrealistic expectation of what life should bring them. And like Rifka, Nicholas takes the challenge and succeeds in becoming a wiser young adult. Will he be put off the ship when found as a stowaway? Will he be able to do the work required—both physically and mentally? Will he ever fit in with the other seamen? With each new challenge he does succeed, so readers know that when he sets off to make amends with his father and the butcher, there will be a successful closure.

What Hannah learns from Klaus and the others in Vermont is the ability to understand and accept their ways. Living with Vashti has been difficult for Hannah because Vashti's ways are not like those to which Hannah is accustomed. Even Tante Rose's explanation of how Vashti was reared doesn't help Hannah's understanding. But living with Klaus and getting to know Miss Carpenter helps Hannah lose her fear of people and things that are different. When she returns to Boston, Hannah is able to better accept both Vashti and Ovadiah.

At the end of *Out of the Dust*, the weather in Oklahoma finally begins to show signs of improvement. Billie Jo's fear for her father's and her livelihood is abated, but another fear takes its place. Billie Jo is afraid of both a life with her father without her mother and her life with her father and another woman. Billie Jo's ability to face these unknowns by recognizing the need for life to continue—hers as well as her father's—helps her overcome these fears.

Nyle is afraid of radiation poisoning and afraid to let herself get involved with someone else who might die. Like so many young adults, Nyle wants assurance that her life won't change; she is afraid of these changes because other changes have caused her so much pain.

Once Leanora decides to tell the truth about Merlin, she begins to lose her fear of the unknown. She realizes that her life will probably not change much when it comes to other people's prejudices, but she also realizes that her ability to focus on herself rather than what people think of her will make her the person she wants to become.

Love and Forgiveness

Hesse says she was a whiny child and remembers getting gold stars on a calendar if she went for a whole day without crying. She continues by saying that it is a testament to the tenacity of love that her family—nuclear and extended—feels any affection for her. Of her extended family—grandparents and aunts—Hesse writes, "I could be weepy, I could be cranky, I could say nothing and they loved me. I felt their unconditional love whenever I was with them. I am sure that at times my aunt and my grandparents wanted to tear their hair out because I was not easy to be with, but I never felt it. I always felt that they loved me no matter what I did."[14] The characters in her books also find this tenacity of unconditional love, but not always in the places one might expect.

Mark Donald was definitely worshiped by his younger sister. She says, "Mark came close to being the perfect brother."[15] In an autobiographical sketch, Hesse speaks fondly of how he would take her to the matinee on weekend afternoons and how patient he was after an afternoon of trampoline jumping when her legs ached too much to walk home. "He encouraged me to sit down on the concrete steps in front of people's homes until I had enough strength to get back up and trudge a few yards further. You'd think after doing this once he'd refuse to take me again, but the next week I was back, begging him to take me jumping and he always agreed."[16]

Her parents, grandparents, aunts, and brother—Hesse knew she had the unconditional love of them all. This unconditional love is also given to the characters in her books, but their love may not always come from the same places as Hesse's.

Billie Jo knows she is loved—by her parents and by many people in the community. Arley and Vera show their love by encouraging her music. Ms. Freeland's love comes as support when Billie Jo needs it most—after her mother's death. And Louise shows her love by letting Billie Jo have time and space to mourn Ma's death. Of Louise, Billie Jo says,

"She knows how to smooth things between two
redheaded people.
And she knows how to come into a home
and not step on the toes of a ghost.
I still feel grateful she didn't make cranberry sauce
last month, at the first Thanksgiving we spent together."[17]

Billie Jo is able to reciprocate this love by accepting Louise into the family.

and wait for Daddy to drive in with Louise
hoping she'll stay a little later,
a little longer,
waiting for the day when she stays for good.[18]

But the person who truly gives Billie Jo unconditional love is her father. In his quiet and patient way he gives Billie Jo the time and space she needs to heal and forgive—both herself and him.

Hannah knows she and her sisters are loved by their parents and by Tante Rose. What surprises her more is the love that Klaus shows her. He brings her into his home and nurses her back to health, and when it is time for her to return to Boston, he gives even more of himself.

From the sugar tin, Uncle Klaus removed four dollar bills.
He handed the money to me.
"I can't take this," I said. "This money was for your hair."
"I cut that hair for you, gal."[19]

Esther is fortunate that her placement in the Fresh Air Program is with Sara Chickering. The lady who has chosen to "manage fine without a man" and is happy because "I'm not a drudge to no one" falls in love with Esther. Sara says,

"I . . . can't imagine life without that child under my feet,
asking a thousand questions
with that odd way of hers,
talking to the animals
and the plants
and the furniture
as if everything
was talking back.
I can't imagine life without that child."[20]

Vera is also fortunate to have a fictive family to take care of her. She goes to Unalaska to live with Alexie and Fekla Golodoff so that she can attend school.

> "'All our childrens are dead,'" the Goldoffs told me.
> "We are old people. We need someone to look out for us.' I clean for them. I carry and chop and fetch for them. I weave fresh grass rugs for them. And they teach me to make things their way, like the seal-gut pants and the seal-gut coats, and they tell me stories every night. We are rich enough and we are happy enough."[21]

But what begins as an arrangement of convenience turns into love. "I try to tell the military that I am not from Kashega, that I am only visiting, that my people, the Golodoffs, are in Unalaska Village and are they okay? And I have to go to them."[22]

Coming of Age

Specialists in human development tell us that puberty is one of the hardest times in a person's life. Not only is the body in a constant state of change, but also emotions are their most volatile. With this confusion comes a time when young adults are trying to find their place in society—with family, peers, and so forth. In Stage 5: Identity versus Role Confusions, regarding this psychosocial development stage, Erik Erickson says that adolescents between the ages of twelve and eighteen are trying to answer the question, "Who am I?"[23] Protagonists in Hesse's stories are doing exactly this. They are struggling to find their own identity while striving to survive in an often hostile environment.

As the stories begin, the protagonists are part of families. In some instances they feel secure with the environment while in other instances they do not. Whether they feel secure or not becomes a moot point when that supportive environment is taken away. Because of the void, they must truly stretch their wings and come of age. This coming of age isn't something that happens overnight or in response to one particular occurrence. Some may think that for Billie Jo it was her mother's death, and this tragedy is a major turning point for her. But struggling to survive hostile weather—both fighting for the crops and at times fighting for her life—helps Billie Jo understand her place in the family and in the community. It is on the train ride to California that she realizes that she can't run away. Finding one's place and being satisfied is one sign of coming of age.

For Rifka, who has always relied on her looks and others for her success, the time on Ellis Island is her coming of age. Once she no longer feels sorry for herself and begins to take responsibility for herself and others, she becomes a person who knows who she is. The realization that she will marry—with or without hair—is a major step toward adulthood, but more important is her realization that she can make a life on her own with or without a husband if she chooses.

Amelia comes to a point where she must choose: follow in her mother's footsteps to please others or do what she really wants to do and go against what society expects. This choice to stay at the lighthouse is not made lightly. She knows that there will be hard work and many obstacles for a woman in a man's profession, but she is willing to make this sacrifice. This choice helps not only her but also others who will follow.

Finding out who you are is not a solitary thing. For each of Hesse's protagonists there is a person (or persons), who helps with the process. For Leonora it's both her father and Mr. Field. Her father encourages her to continue her education, knowing that this will enable her to avoid the type of life he has had to live. It is Mr. Field, who is blind, who makes her truly understand that skin color is of no importance. He encourages her to do what's right about Merlin Van Tornhout. And making the decision to tell the truth helps her to understand who she really is—which has nothing to do with skin color.

Hannah may be the character who changes the least in respect to coming of age. At fourteen she is already the mother figure for her two younger sisters. She also feels responsibility to help Tante Rose, since Hannah and her sisters must live with their aunt in their parents' absence. Hannah has already taken on the responsibility of a job—selling newspapers—but still feels obligated to help Tante Rose with the sewing at night. What changes for Hannah is her insight into the world and its other inhabitants. Having grown up in a Jewish neighborhood with Jewish traditions, it is difficult for her to accept people who are not like she is. Her distrust of Klaus—his heritage, his food, and his desire to help her—is obvious. Having lived in a tight-knit community with people of a similar background, she is taken back by the friendliness of the strangers she meets. Their acceptance of her makes Hannah realize that she must be more accepting of others. Ovadiah and Vashti are the recipients of this newfound empathy.

Nyle's realization that death is a natural progression of life helps her to find out who she is and thus come of age. A person who had been afraid of the "dying room," Nyle can now sit with Ezra in his last minutes and when asked, even give him the physical comfort he needs.

"I stroked the fine bone of his skull. Then I touched the craggy eyes; his bones felt so fragile, so close to the surface."[24]
Ezra's eyelids shut and he trembled. A hint of deep purple showed beneath his lids.
"I'm tired," he said.
"I know."
"Nyle, I have to leave."
"I know that too, Ezra."
"You'll be okay?"
"Ayuh."[25]

Mila's coming of age may be in the final chapter of the book when she chooses to return to the dolphins. The choice is a difficult one, but she makes the decision to return to the only family she has truly known. When Hesse's editor asked that she rewrite the ending, Hesse had to go back and restructure the story so that Mila chooses to stay with human society. But it wasn't true—the new ending or the story that led up to it—so Hesse chose to stay with the original ending, in which Mila returns to the dolphins. As readers we are torn about which decision would be the best for her. But as with her other books, Hesse stays with what is true rather that what might make her readers (or editors) feel most comfortable. For this determination her readers say, "It wasn't some perfect ending. It was real."[26] (This statement was made in reference to *Out of the Dust*, but it works for all of Hesse's books.)

For Vera and Nicholas, growing up comes much earlier than for some of Hesse's other characters. Both Vera and Nicholas lose a parent and their homes at an early age. Vera is sent away—albeit to attend school—as is Nicholas in order to rid the parent of an unwanted nuisance. Vera is fortunate to have a supportive culture. The Aleuts as a community take care of each other, but for Nicholas there is no community. When her people are relocated from their island home to the mainland, Vera must suffer hardships with the others; but it is not until she returns home to see the devastation and her beloved home, that she begins to feel as though she has come of age. She realizes that it is up to her and the other survivors to rebuild their own lives. Prior to this revelation she has been comfortable letting others take the responsibility, but now she sees it as her job to continue the Aleut way of life for future generations.

Nicholas suffers great hardships—physical, mental, and emotional, but he doesn't really come of age until he makes peace with himself. Knowing that once the voyage is over he must face his nemeses—his father and the butcher—shows how much he has matured over the three years. From the other seamen on the voyage, it's obvious that the voyage alone does not make a person mature; it is what that person gets out of his experiences that matures him.

Forging Relationships That Last

In her autobiographical works Hesse talks about friends she's had for years. She talks about family relationships that don't include hyphenated titles. She talks about relationships that last. The characters in her books also have these types of relationships. These relationships may be teenager to teenager, girl to girl or girl to boy, or they may be between teenager and adult. They may be friend to friend, or they may be family to family. But there are always relationships, and many of these relationships last—just as Hesse's have.

In *Phoenix Rising* Nyle and Muncie have a typical teenage relationship. It's an on-again off-again friendship that endures all types of disagreements. Their friendship may have begun because of physical proximity—Muncie's parents live in one of Gran's rental houses on the farm—but their friendship has evolved into true caring for each other. The reader quickly realizes that Nyle's friendship with Ezra won't last in the physical sense because he will die, but that the impact he has on Nyle will last. This may be why Hesse originally titled the book *Forever Ezra*.

For Vera, Hannah, Billie Jo, and Amelia one type of friendship that lasts is with the opposite sex and may be referred to as girlfriend–boyfriend situations. Hesse didn't set out to write romantic novels, and the stories of these friendships—even though romance plays a role—are about relationships that will last—not a teenage crush. There is the initial infatuation, but in the telling of her stories Hesse shows the reader how true lasting relationships are formed through common interests and shared goals, through everyday struggles and joys, and through caring for and being cared about.

Vera and Alfred have been a part of each other's lives since early childhood.

> I was six when I stood outside Alfred's grandfather's house, where the old ways steep like tea in a cup of hours. Alfred's mother opened the door and gazed down at my small fists hanging by my sides. She understood my wanting. She said I could live in her house sometimes if I needed.[27]

Unlike her mother and her friend Pari, Vera likes the old ways. This, she and Alfred have in common. The struggles of the relocation camp are a second bond they share, but the caring Alfred shows for Vera's grief at the sight of her once beloved home may be the most important bond of all.

Hannah and Harry have grown up together in the Jewish area of Boston. They share a common neighborhood and a common culture. Being Jewish in Boston in the early 1900s makes their families different from others, but helps to form a closer bond between them. Hannah and Harry also take responsibility for their families. As the oldest, Hannah feels responsible for Libby and Eve after their parents leave; Harry becomes the man of the family after the death of his father. A mutual bond is formed that the reader realizes will eventually become romantic love.

Billie Jo and Mad Dog Craddock must survive the Oklahoma Dust Bowl. Typical of teens in any era or location is the competition that comes with wanting to succeed in a chosen field. For Billie Jo and Mad Dog that chosen field is music: she a pianist, and he a vocalist. Yet they are constantly vying for the attention, accolades, and financial gains that might come with their talents. Their music helps them survive the stark and cruel world of the dirty thirties, and the music brings them together to compete and cheer for each other. Once Billie Jo makes peace with her father, she is content to stay on the farm in Oklahoma and "wait for Mad Dog when he comes past once a week on his way from Amarillo, where he works for the radio."[28]

For Amelia her relationship is with Daniel Worthington. Daniel has always been a part of her life, but it is through their grieving after the death of his brother that they truly begin to care for each other. Relationships that last are built on mutual respect and admiration. Daniel demonstrates the deepening relationship when he helps Amelia with her chores at the lighthouse rather than wanting her to take on a more "feminine" role. Daniel truly understands her, as she does him. Amelia understands his need to be a part of the solution to the conflict that arose because of slavery.

Leanora's relationship with Mr. Field begins as employer-employee—he needs someone to help him. But what this wise man—even though he's blind—brings to Leanora is understanding and compassion for others.

> but then mr. field said,
> leanora, no way to pay a debt
> by stealing from someone else to do it.
>
> he's pretty smart, mr. field

for a skinny, half-blind, old white man.[29]

Hesse's readers know that Leanora and Mr. Field have bonded and that they will be there to help each other through many trials.

Notes

1. Ellen Huntington Bryant, "Honoring the Complexities of Our Lives: An Interview with Karen Hesse," *Voices from the Middle* 4, no. 2 (1997): 41.

2. Karen Hesse, *Out of the Dust* (NY: Scholastic Press, 1997), 3.

3. Karen Hesse, *A Light in the Storm: The Civil War Diary of Amelia Martin* (NY: Scholastic Inc., 1999), 135.

4. Karen Hesse, *The Music of Dolphins* (NY: Scholastic Signature, 1996), 137.

5. Alan Hedblad, ed. "Karen Hesse," in *Something about the Author* 113. (Farmington, MI: Gale Group, 2000), 78.

6. Karen Hesse, *Out of the Dust*, 227.

7. Karen Hesse, *Letters from Rifka* (NY: Puffin Books/ Penguin Putnam, 1992), 138.

8. Karen Hesse, *Stowaway* (NY: Simon and Schuster, 2000), 300.

9. Karen Hesse, *A Time of Angels* (NY: Hyperion, 1995), 38.

10. Karen Hesse, *A Time of Angels*, 23.

11. Karen Hesse, *Aleutian Sparrow* (NY: Simon and Schuster, 2003), 149.

12. Karen Hesse, *The Music of Dolphins*, 179.

13. Karen Hesse, *Aleutian Sparrow*, 153.

14. Ellen Huntington Bryant, *Voices from the Middle*, 41.

15. Alan Hedblad, "Karen Hesse," 70.

16. Alan Hedblad, "Karen Hesse," 70.

17. Karen Hesse, *Out of the Dust*, 224.

18. Karen Hesse, *Out of the Dust*, 227.

19. Karen Hesse, *A Time of Angels*, 207.

20. Karen Hesse, *Witness* (NY: Scholastic Press, 2001), 61.

21. Karen Hesse, *Aleutian Sparrow*, 16.

22. Karen Hesse, *Aleutian Sparrow*, 19.

23. Erik Erikson, *Identity: Youth and Crisis*, (NY: Norton, 1968), 128-135.

24. Karen Hesse, *Phoenix Rising* (NY: Puffin Books/Penguin Putnam, 1994), 180.

25. Karen Hesse, *Phoenix Rising*, 180.

26. Literature Learning Ladders Classroom Connections website. www.eduscapes.com/newbery/98a.html, April 7, 2003.

27. Karen Hesse, *Aleutian Sparrow*, 13.

28. Karen Hesse, *Out of the Dust*, 219.

29. Karen Hesse, *Witness*, 160.

Chapter 5

Books for Younger Readers

One of Karen Hesse's strengths is the ability to write for all age groups. She says that when a book is in its beginning, she doesn't know the audience—she lets the topic and context of the book make this decision. (*A Time of Angels* began as a manuscript for a picture book but turned into a novel, thanks to her editor's wanting more information about Hannah and her life.)

Her books for younger readers include picture books, chapter books for beginning readers, and transition chapter books for the intermediate grades. *Poppy's Chair*, *Lester's Dog*, *Come On, Rain*, and *The Cats of Krasinski Square* (to be published in the fall of 2004) are the picture books. *The Stone Lamp: Eight Stories of Hanukkah through History* is in the picture book format but is enjoyed by older readers. *Lavender* and *Sable* are chapter books for the beginning reader while *Wish on a Unicorn* and *Just Juice* are for intermediate readers. These books—like those for her adolescent readers—show strong characters who gain a sense of responsibility, overcome their fears, and develop a better understanding of and appreciation for themselves and their families. As these protagonists struggle with adversity—and sometimes loss—they gain stronger and richer personalities.

Of course, these books can be enjoyed by older readers as well. In a *Language Arts* article in 1999 a group of teachers (Cathy Beck, Linda Gwyn, Dick Koblitz, Anne O'Connor, Kathryn Mitchell Pierce, and Susan Wolf) write about a series of literature discussions they instigated. They asked a group of teachers to read several of Hesse's books for an adult literature discussion group. They also shared these same books with their students ranging in age from six to fourteen years of age. "We were struck by the fact that our children discussed the same themes that we had discussed in our adult discussion group."[1] This conclusion seems to validate a quote by J. Donald Adams who said, "I have nothing but respect for writers of good books for children; they perform one of the most admirable functions of which a writer is capable. One proof of their value is the fact that the greatest books which children can enjoy are read with equal delight by their elders."[2] Hesse's books for younger readers—like those for young adults—are delightful for all readers.

Wish on a Unicorn

Hesse's first book was *Wish on a Unicorn* about a family who is poor in material goods but wealthy in the love they have for each other. It is in this book that Hesse drew from her background of being a "collection man's" daughter. Mags (Margaret Wade), Hannie, and Moochie live in a rundown trailer with their mom. Mags is a sixth grader at the time in her life when being popular means everything. But instead of being able to be friends with Patty Jo and Alice, she has to take care of eight-year-old Hannie—who is mentally challenged—and six-year-old Moochie—the typical feisty, always-in-trouble younger brother.

Mags knows the stuffed unicorn she and Hannie find can't be magic, but a series of coincidences in which wishes seem to be granted makes her question this logic. What Mags learns from Hannie, the unicorn, and a wish-fulfilled afternoon with the popular girls is that "maybe everything we always wish for is waiting somewhere, waiting for us to catch up and make it come true."[3]

This unicorn made Hesse's wishes come true in that it was her flagship book. Brenda Bowen remembers reading the original manuscript of *Wish on a Unicorn*. It was only four pages long, but the first sentence "Hannie and I were walking home from school when we saw a unicorn in Newell's field,"[4] intrigued her. Bowen immediately liked the story but wanted to know more about "the characters, the situation, the magic." When asked if Hesse could revise, the response was definitely in the affirmative. *Wish on a Unicorn* was published, and Hesse's illustrious career as a writer for children and young adults began.

Poppy's Chair

Growing up in a family where each person has separate chairs—like the Three Bears—seems to be typical. Hesse must have had this experience also, because she uses the grandfather's chair as the pivotal point in the book *Poppy's Chair*. The first time Leah visits her grandparents' home after Poppy's death, she has trouble dealing with the chair. "Gramm and Leah curl up on the silky sofa. . . . Neither of them sit in Poppy's chair. Leah hasn't gone near Poppy's chair since he died."[5] It's not only the chair, but Leah also remembers everything that she and Poppy did together, from picking out charms for her bracelet to sneaking samples of Gramm's cooking, and she is very sad. With Gramm's words of wisdom Leah learns to bring back the good memories of Poppy. "But sooner or later, you'll let those awful feelings go. Then you'll have room for the good feelings to come back again."[6]

Hesse says she drew on her own childhood visits with her grandparents in creating this story. She even used their house as the house in the story. In one of her autobiographical pieces Hesse talks about loving to go through her grandmother's jewelry boxes, and she has Leah do the same thing in *Poppy's Chair*. "While Gramm is dressing, Leah sorts through Gramm's jewelry box. She sits on the edge of Gramm's bed and untangles a bracelet with big yellow roses."[7]

Hesse realizes that young children must deal with death of loved ones, and she is helping them through this process with *Poppy's Chair*.

Lavender

Poppy's Chair was followed by a young reader semi-autobiographical chapter book that also deals with learning to accept changes in the family. Codie and her Aunt Alix have a very special relationship—much like Karen and her Aunt Bern. Aunt Alix is expecting, and Codie is both excited and a bit jealous. She's excited about her new cousin, but also wonders if Aunt Alix will have as much time for her when the baby arrives.

Codie wants to give her first cousin a special present, so she decides to make a blanket from the scrap basket. The blanket is to be a surprise for Aunt Alix and the new baby, and Codie manages to finish it just in time for Lavender's arrival. The long-awaited meeting of her new cousin finally arrives, and at first, Codie is disappointed in this red, wrinkly, and bald thing in the crib. But once Codie gets to hold the baby—who is wrapped in the blanket she made—she thinks the baby is "lovely."

Once again Hesse shows that she understands her readers and their need for feeling included. Whether it is a new cousin, or a new baby brother or sister, children need reassurance that their place in the family unit is secure and special.

Lester's Dog

The same year that *Poppy's Chair* and *Lavender* were published so was *Lester's Dog*. This picture book, like the chapter book *Wish on a Unicorn*, deals with a child's ability to overcome fears. For the narrator in *Lester's Dog*, it is a dog that is feared. In order to find out what Corey wants to show him, our narrator has to go "up the hill, to the top of Garrison Avenue,"[8] which means that he'll have to pass Lester's dog—the dog that had bitten him on the nose when he was six years old.

Trying to explain his fears to Corey doesn't work "'cause he can't hear you, and even if he could he's too stubborn to listen."[9] So the two boys go up the hill, past Lester's house, but the dog is "too busy digging dust under his porch to notice me and Corey."[10] Corey, who can't hear, has somehow discovered a small kitten trapped in a cellar and wants to rescue it. They must now pass Lester's house again on their way back down the hill, but this time with a kitten. Like Mags in *Wish on a Unicorn*, our narrator overcomes his fear of Lester's dog—not to keep himself safe but to save the kitten. "All the times I've been scared is all bundled into right now. But suddenly what I'm feeling is not scared. What I'm feeling is mad."[11]

"A rumbling starts deep in my throat. I glare into that dog's face, and a sound rises up from a place inside of me I didn't know was there. My whole body fills with the sound and the ground seems to shake under me as I roar at Lester's dog."[12]

"And Lester's dog is backing off. He's leaving, whining, and slinking all the way up the block, crawling on his belly to hide under Lester's porch."[13]

Hesse is again telling her readers that they have—inside themselves—the ability to take care of themselves and others. (*Lester's Dog* is the only one of Hesse's books that is not currently in print.)

Sable

This transition chapter book for young readers tells the story of ten-year-old Tate Marshall and Sable. Tate "had no hope of getting a dog" because "Mam would not hear about having a dog. She didn't like them, none of them."[14] So when a stray comes to their house, Tate begins a campaign to keep "Sable"—so named because of the texture of her fur. The first week is great, but then Sable begins to leave during the day; then she begins to bring other peoples' belongings to the yard, and finally the neighbors begin to complain. Chaining Sable doesn't work—she's smart enough to get loose, so Pap decides to give her away to Doc Winston, who has a big fenced yard. Tate is devastated and thinks building a fence in their yard will convince her parents to let Sable return. It takes Tate several weeks to build the fence, but she goes to Doc Wilson's to retrieve the dog only to find out that Sable has run away.

Tate is a typical Hesse character—a strong-minded, independent person who doesn't accept failure or defeat. In order to feed Sable, Tate is willing to dust and sweep at the store in exchange for dog food. When it becomes apparent that Sable has to be kept in a fenced area, Tate takes it upon herself to build the fence. But the main characteristic of Tate, and all of Hesse's protagonists, is their ability never to give up hope.

Tate hopes the fence will allow her to bring Sable home, and in a way it does. The storm that blows down power lines and tree limbs doesn't blow down Tate's fence. So when Sable runs away from Doc Winston's and makes her journey back to the Marshall's, the fence is waiting for her.

Come on, Rain

Two years after *Out of the Dust* was published and one year after it won the Newbery medal, the book that began the Dust Bowl project came into print. *Come on, Rain* was the manuscript that caused Eileen Christelow to ask the question, "Why do these children want it to rain so much?"

We know the answer to that question thanks to *Out of the Dust*, but *Come On, Rain*, is still a delight to read.

Tessie narrates her own story about a wonderful summer day; all that the children need to make it perfect is rain so that they can play in it. Like in *Out of the Dust*, Hesse makes her readers feel the heat and humidity of a hot summer day. The vines are listless; the plants are parched; and Tessie is sizzling like a hot potato. But she sees the "clouds rolling in, gray clouds, bunched and bulging under a purple sky."[15]

The neighborhood children "meet in the alleyway. All the insects have gone still. Trees sway under a swollen sky, the wind grows bold and bolder, . . . and just like that, rain comes."[16] The children have had the foresight to put on bathing suits, but "we make such a racket, Miz Glick rushes out on her porch." Miz Grace and Miz Vera soon follow, and then Mamma joins the group. "Leaning over their rails, they turn to each other. A smile spreads from porch to porch. And with a wordless nod . . . first one, then all . . . fling off their shoes, skim off their hose, tossing streamers of stockings over their shoulders. Our barelegged mammas dance down the steps and join us in the fresh, clean rain"[17]

As this book is read, visions of West Garrison Avenue come to mind. Mrs. Donald and the other mothers probably didn't join in the revelry, but this celebration would have been a child's fantasy. Hesse acknowledges that the topic for this book comes from her wonderful childhood experiences.

Just Juice

In her second chapter book for intermediate readers, Hesse tells the story of nine-year-old Juice Faulstich. Juice must face the poverty of her family as well as the stigma of not being able to read. The middle of five sisters, Juice believes herself to be stupid and is embarrassed to go to school. But when the family is faced with losing their home because of unpaid back taxes and Ma goes into labor early, Juice is the resourceful one who knows what to do.

Hesse again shows her readers how they can have a significant influence on their own lives as well as the lives of people around them. As with Mags in *Wish on a Unicorn*, Hesse shows the love of family and how this affection can make a difference in any socioeconomic status.

The Stone Lamp: Eight Stories of Hanukkah through History

For her latest book Hesse has tried yet another format for her writing. *The Stone Lamp* is a collection of short stories done in the picture book genre, but it is also a nonfiction book about the persecutions of Jews throughout the centuries. The first page gives a brief description of the origins of Hanukkah, the midwinter festival of lights, which began in 164 BCE when Judah Maccabee reclaimed Jerusalem for the Jews.

Then beginning with the Crusades, there are eight historical accounts of Jewish persecution: from York, England and the burning of Clifford Tower; to Kristallnacht in Graz, Austria; to the assassination of Yitzhak Rabin in Tel Aviv, Israel. Each of the eight historical summaries is accompanied by a short story telling of the lighting of the Hanukkah candles by people who would have lived during that era.

This book is Hesse's first attempt to go back to her Jewish roots, and she has done a wonderful job. But each of the eight stories also illuminates the choices that people make and their ability to overcome all odds and stand up for their beliefs. This theme seems to run through all of Hesse's books. She definitely wants her readers to realize that they can make a difference by their choices in life.

Notes

1. Cathy Beck, Linda Gwyn, Dick Koblitz, Anne O'Connor, Kathryn Mitchell Pierce, and Susan Wolf, "Talking About Books: Karen Hesse," *Language Arts* 76 (January 1999): 264.

2. Donald Adams, *Speaking of Books and Life*, ed. Holt, Rinehart, and Winston (1965): 251-252.

3. Karen Hesse, *Wish on a Unicorn* (NY: Puffin Books/Penguin Putnam Books, 1991), 40.

4. Karen Hesse, *Wish on a Unicorn*, 1.

5. Karen Hesse, *Poppy's Chair* (NY: Scholastic Inc., 2000).

6. Karen Hesse, *Poppy's Chair*.

7. Karen Hesse, *Poppy's Chair*.

8. Karen Hesse, *Lester's Dog* (NY: Knopf Books for Young Readers, 1993).

9. Karen Hesse, *Lester's Dog*.

10. Karen Hesse, *Lester's Dog*.

11. Karen Hesse, *Lester's Dog*.

12. Karen Hesse, *Lester's Dog*.

13. Karen Hesse, *Sable* (NY: Henry Holt and Company, 1998).

14. Karen Hesse, *Come On, Rain* (NY: Scholastic Press, 1999).

15. Karen Hesse, *Come On, Rain*.

16. Karen Hesse, *Come On, Rain*.

17. Karen Hesse, *Come On, Rain*.

Chapter 6

Conclusion

What's to Come

Hesse is presently working on two manuscripts, one of which will be out in the fall of 2004—before this book is printed. This picture book, titled *The Cats in Krasinski Square*, is set in Poland. Hesse says she got the idea for this latest book while doing research for *Aleutian Sparrow*.

Set in Warsaw during World War II, this wonderful story tells about the Jewish Resistance and their plan to get food to the people starving in the Ghetto. Stray cats and people with a desire to help those who can't help themselves combine to foil an attack by the Gestapo. In order to get food to the Jews in the Ghetto, the Resistance devises a plan where people from all over Poland will come into Warsaw on one particular train. Each passenger will have in his satchels—not clothes—but food to be smuggled into the Ghetto. When the Gestapo finds out about the plan, the narrator—who like Rifka is Jewish but can pass for Gentile—suggests a plan. The Gestapo is intending to meet the train with dogs who can sniff out the food. Then the people carrying the food can be arrested, and the food will not get to the Ghetto. But the stray cats in Krasinski Square are used as decoys to distract the dogs, and the food is safely delivered to those who desperately need it.

After *The Cats in Krasinski Square*, Hesse's readers can look forward to a book about the early years of Hans Christian Andersen. Still in the research stage, the format and title of this book is yet to be decided.

Conclusion

Mark Twain so aptly says, "The difference between the right word and the almost right word is the difference between lightning and the lightning bug."

With Hesse and her writing it is definitely the lightning. As Randy Hesse is a craft person with wood, Karen Hesse is a craft person with words. In talking about her writing, reviewers use phrases such as "fluid and graceful use of figurative language," "skillful crafting of dialogue," "lyrical," "as moving as a sonnet," and "similes shine like jewels in a dark cave."

Most of her readers don't consciously recognize her skills as a wordsmith. What they do recognize is her great storytelling ability. So Hesse continues to educate her readers by exposing them to fine writing.

Hodding Carter said, "There are only two lasting bequests we can hope to give our children. One of these is roots, the other wings."[1]

Hesse does both of these with her books. Showing young readers the history and heritage of their lives gives them the roots they need in order to grow. Their wings come with the realization that—like Hesse's protagonists—they have control over their choices and decisions.

Note

1. Karen Hesse, "Newbery Medal Acceptance," *Horn Book Magazine* 74, no. 4 (July/August 1998).

Bibliography

Books by Karen Hesse

A Light in the Storm: The Civil War Diary of Amelia Martin. NY: Scholastic Inc., 1999.

A Time of Angels. NY: Hyperion, 1995.

Aleutian Sparrow. NY: Simon and Schuster, 2003.

The Cats in Krasinski Square. NY: Scholastic Press, 2004.

Come On, Rain. NY: Scholastic Press, 1999.

Just Juice. NY: Scholastic Signature, 1998.

Lavender. NY: Henry Holt and Company, 1993.

Lester's Dog. NY: Knopf Books for Young Readers, 1993.

Letters from Rifka. NY: Puffin Books/Penguin Putnam, 1992.

The Music of Dolphins. NY: Scholastic Signature, 1996.

Out of the Dust. NY: Scholastic Press, 1997.

Phoenix Rising. NY: Puffin Books/Penguin Putnam, 1994.

Poppy's Chair. NY: Scholastic Inc., 2000.

Sable. NY: Henry Holt and Company, 1998.

The Stone Lamp: Eight Stories of Hanukkah through History. NY: Hyperion Books for Children, 2003.

Stowaway. NY: Simon and Schuster, 2000.

Wish on a Unicorn. NY: Puffin Books/Penguin Putnam Books, 1991.

Witness. NY: Scholastic Press, 2001.

Other Sources

Adams, Donald. *Speaking of Books and Life*, ed. Holt, Rinehart, and Winston. (1965): 251–252.

ALA News release. January 1998. www.ala.org/news/majorawards. html. February 10, 2003.

Andriani, Lynn. "Review of the Book *Witness*." *Publisher's Weekly* 248, no. 42 (October 2001): 26.

Anonymous. "Review of the Book *Aleutian Sparrow*." *Publisher's Weekly* 250, no. 38 (September 2003): 104.

Beck, Cathy, Linda Gwyn, Dick Koblitz, Anne O'Connor, Kathryn Mitchell Pierce, and Susan Wolf. "Talking about Books: Karen Hesse." *Language Arts* 76 (January 1999): 263–271.

Bowen, Brenda. "Karen Hesse." *Horn Book Magazine* 74, no. 4. (July/August 1998): 428–432.

Breem, Karen, Ellen Fader, Kathleen Odear, and Zena Sutherland. "One Hundred Books That Shaped the Century." *School Library Journal* 46, no. 1 (January 2000): 50–58.

Bryant, Ellen Huntington. "Honoring the Complexities of Our Lives: An Interview with Karen Hesse." *Voices from the Middle* 4, no. 2 (1997): 38–49.

Cooper, Ilene. "Story behind the Story: Hesse's *The Stone Lamp*." *Booklist* (October 2003): 335.

Devereaux, Elizabeth. "Karen Hesse: Apoetics of Perfectionism." *Publisher's Weekly* 246, no. 6 (February 1999): 190–191.

Erikson, Erik. *Identity: Youth and Crisis*. New York: Norton, 1968. 128–135.

Fischer, Marc David. "Humanity and Hate: An Interview with Newbery Award-winning Author Karen Hesse." *Scholastic Scope* 50, no. 12 (February 2002): 12–15.

Glenn, Wendy. "Consider the Source: Feminism and Point of View in Karen Hesse's *Stowaway* and *Witness*." *The ALAN Review* 30 no. 2 (2003): 30–34.

———. "Form Follows Function." *The ALAN Review* 31 no 2. (2004): 27–31.

Hedblad, Alan, ed. "Karen Hesse." 80–86 in *Something about the Author* 103. Farmington, MI: Gale Group, 1999.

———. "Karen Hesse." 67–82 in *Something about the Author* 113. Farmington, MI: Gale Group, 2000.

Hendershot, Judy, and Jackie Peck. "Newbery Medal Winner, Karen Hesse, Brings Billie Jo's Voice *Out of the Dust*." *The Reading Teacher* 52 (1999): 856–858.

Heppermann, Christine M. "Review of the Book *Witness.*" *Horn Book Magazine* 77, no. 6 (November/December 2001): 749.

Hesse, Karen. "Newbery Medal Acceptance." *Horn Book Magazine* 74, no. 4 (July/August 1998): 422–427.

———. "Unforgettable Teachers: Thank You, Mr. Ball." *Instructor (Primary Edition)* 108, no. 5 (January/February 1999): 86–87.

———. "Waiting for Midnight." *When I Was Your Age: Original Stories about Growing Up* 2nd ed. Amy Ehrlich. Cambridge, MA: Candlewick Press, 1996.

———. "Waiting for Midnight." *When I Was Your Age: Original Stories about Growing Up* 2nd ed. Amy Ehrlich. Cambridge, MA: Candlewick Press, 1999.

———. "Waiting for Midnight." *When I Was Your Age: Original Stories about Growing Up* 2nd ed. Amy Ehrlich. Cambridge, MA: Candlewick Press, 2002.

Hipple, Ted, and Amy Maupin. "What's Good about the Best?" *English Journal* 90, no. 3 (2001): 40-42.

"Interview with Leonard Marcus." *Listening Library.*

"Karen Hesse." *Educational Paperback Association.* 2001, www.edu-paper-back.org/authorbios/Hesse_Karen.html (12 September 2001)

"Karen Hesse." *Eighth Book of Junior Authors and Illustrators.* Ed. Connie C. Rockman. NY: H.W. Wilson Company, 2000. 216–219.

"Karen Hesse." KidsReads.com. 2001. www.Kidsreads.com/authors /au-hesse-karen.asp.

"Karen Hesse." Meet Authors and Illustrators. www.childrenslit.com

"Karen Hesse: 1998 Newbery Award Winner." Brooks Memorial Library www.state.vt.us/libraries/b733/BrooksLibrary.featured_author.htm.

"Karen Hesse Awarded MacArthur Fellowship." Simon & Schuster Publishing Press Release. (Sept 25, 2002).

"Karen Hesse's Interview Transcript." Scholastic. www.scholastic.com/teachers/authorsandbooks/authorstudies/authorhome.jhtml.

Kirkus Reviews, (August 2001).

Lempke, Susan Dove. "Review of *Out of the Dust.*" *Booklist* 94 (1997): 330.

"Let's Talk about *Witness.*" Scholastic. http://teacher.scholastic.com/authorsandbooks/events/hesse/Karen_Hesse_transcript.htm.

McLoughlin, William. *School Library Journal* 46, no. 11 (2000): 156.

Merriam-Webster's Collegiate Dictionary, 10th ed.

O'Malley, Judy. "Talking with . . . Karen Hesse." Book Links 9 no. 1 (September 1999): 54-57.

Oluonye, Mary N. "Review of the Book *Aleutian Sparrow.*" *School Library Journal* 49, no. 10 (October 2003): 166–167.

Publisher's Weekly 244, no. 35 (1997): 72

Publisher's Weekly 247, no. 43 (2000): 75.

Roback, Diane, Jennifer M. Brown, and Jason Britton. "Review of the Book *Witness*." *Publisher's Weekly* 248, no. 34 (August 2001): 80–81.

Rochman, Hazel. "Review of the Book *Witness*." *Booklist* 98, no. 1 (September 2001): 108.

Scholastic Online Reading Club, http://teacher.scholastic.com/ authorsandbooks/events/hesse/Karen_Hesse_transcript.htm, (14 November 2002).

Stover, Lois T. "Karen Hesse." *Writers for Young Adults*. Ed. Ted Hipple. New York: Charles Schribners and Sons, 2000. 93-101.

Welty, Ellen. "Writing Their Own Fairy Tale." *Good Housekeeping* 236, no. 2 (February 2003): 85.

Whelan, Debra Lau. "Karen Hesse Awarded MacArthur Fellowship." *School Library Journal* 48, no. 11 (November 2002): 23.

Unless otherwise cited, information and quotations from Karen Hesse come from interviews, telephone conversations, and personal correspondence with the author.

Index

About the Author

Rosemary Oliphant-Ingham is associate professor and coordinator of secondary education at the University of Mississippi where she teaches courses in children's and adolescent literature as well as secondary English methods. Prior to coming to Ole Miss, she taught at Belmont University (Nashville, TN), University of Houston-Clear Lake (Texas), Northern Kentucky University, University of Houston (Texas) and in public schools in Tennessee, Georgia, and Texas. She holds a bachelor of arts in education from Western Kentucky University, a masters of education from the University of Mississippi, and her doctorate from the University of Houston. She has served on the board of directors for ALAN (Adolescent Literature Assembly Network of NCTE), SIGNAL (Special Interest Group Network on Adolescent Literature), and has been an active member of NCTE, IRA, and their state affiliates. She has contributed chapters to three books dealing with adolescent literature, two volumes of *Books for You*, and published in various journals. Reading, traveling, and spending time with family (nuclear, extended, and fictive) makes up her leisure time.